Managing Open Systems

Open and Distance Learning Series

Series Editor: Fred Lockwood

Managing Open Systems

RICHARD FREEMAN

**KOGAN
PAGE**

London • Stirling (USA)

Published in association with the
Institute of Educational Technology, Open University

First published in 1997

Kogan Page Limited
120 Pentonville Road
London N1 9JN
and
22883 Quicksilver Drive
Stirling, VA 20166, USA

British Library Cataloguing in Publication Data

A CIP record for this book is available from the British Library.

ISBN 0 7494 2056 1

Typeset by JS Typesetting, Wellingborough, Northants.
Printed and bound in Great Britain by Biddles Ltd, Guildford and King's Lynn

Contents

Acknowledgements

I am grateful to Dr Fred Lockwood and Professor Roger Lewis for their helpful advice on earlier drafts of this work. Such errors and omissions that remain are, however, my responsibility alone.

I am grateful to the following for their kind permission to reproduce examples as below:

Example 1 Pre-enrolment information: National Westminster Bank

Example 2 The use of a computer to provide pre-course study guidance: University of Lincolnshire and Humberside

Example 3 A tutor biography: National Extension College

Example 4 A course timetable: National Police Training

Example 5 Advice on how to study open learning materials: National Extension College

Example 6 Advice to learners on building their portfolios: National Police Training

Example 7 An enrolment form for a distance learning course: National Extension College

Example 8 Learning materials on the Internet: University of Colorado

Example 9 A course Internet site which provides access to other Internet learning resources: University of Monash

Example 10 Part of the Poetica home page: University of Sunderland

Example 11 More of the Poetica home page: University of Sunderland

Example 12 The layered structure of a hypertext course: Charlie Mansfield and Suzanne Robertson

Example 13 A model for Internet course design: Charlie Mansfield and Suzanne Robertson

Example 14 A distance learning kit: Society of Cosmetic Scientists

Series editor's foreword

There are numerous books available that attempt to provide an overview of producing self-instructional material in open, distance and flexible learning contexts. There are also many books that focus upon one or more elements that contribute to these systems. However, there is a marked absence of books that address the fundamental questions of managing such learning systems. *Managing Open Systems* by Richard Freeman fills this gap with distinction. In assembling it Richard has done all of us involved in the provision of self-instructional material, not just managers, a great service.

Successful open learning initiatives seldom happen by chance; they are dependent upon careful management – on planning, organization, motivation and control. Richard acknowledges these four functions and offers a framework within which to consider all open learning systems. The framework combines three alternatives of *where learners wish to study* with two alternatives of whether the *learning is self-paced or group-paced*. The resultant six categories of open learning system offer a simple but extremely effective framework in which to consider his subsequent chapters.

There can be few people in the world with more experience than Richard Freeman of both large and small open and distance learning systems. His managerial contribution to the success of The Open College is well known, as is his wider contribution to, and knowledge of, this growing area of teaching and training. This is evident in the numerous examples that Richard draws upon to illustrate the points he makes. I have seldom seen a book that managed to contain so many examples and combined these with case studies and checklists into a balanced whole. They contribute to an engaging book and represent a superb resource.

At the outset Richard admits to a pragmatic approach and to the hope that the ideas, suggestions and arguments he offers will enable you to apply them to any learning system or to create your own. You will be the judge. However, I am sure that after reading this book you will feel confident in your ability to do so.

Fred Lockwood

Chapter 1

Introduction

What counts as an open learning system?

Definitions of open and flexible learning vary, but they tend to have one common theme: some degree of learner control over when, where or what is learnt. I do not wish to tie this book to a narrow interpretation of just what an open learning system is. Rather, I hope that people starting new systems will be able to decide for themselves whether they can adapt the methods that others have used. So, pragmatically, I shall look at the management of any system where learners are substantially responsible for their own learning but are still formally enrolled in a system which includes other learners. So, at one extreme I shall exclude learners who just borrow books from the local library or surf the Internet and, at the other extreme, I shall exclude lecture-based courses where the limit of self-organized learning is choosing when to write one's weekly essay.

Learners and students

I have used both 'learners' and 'students' to describe those who study within the systems discussed in this book. I have used the word 'student' where the text would otherwise read oddly, generally, however, I have used the term 'learner'.

Examples and figures

The text contains both examples and figures. All the examples are taken from open systems which were teaching at the time of writing. The figures are other illustrative material, either specially created for the book or taken from sources other than open systems.

Types of systems

There are a number of ways in which open systems can be categorized. From the point of view of the management of open systems, there are two dimensions that help to identify categories with similar problems and, sometimes, similar solutions.

The first dimension concerns where the learners live and work in relation to the organization that is providing the service. Systems can be categorized into three broad groupings on this dimension:

- systems where the learners are all on one site (or can easily travel to the one site), eg campus-based flexible and open learning schemes such as those at the Universities of Sunderland and Lincolnshire and Humberside
- systems where the learners are all in one organization, even if the organization is widely scattered, eg the National Westminster Bank
- systems where learners are isolated with no work or social links between them, eg distance learning students at the Open University.

The second key dimension that affects management systems is whether or not learners are free to study at their own pace. Where learners are not, then learner cohorts can be formed and events such as tutorials and exams can be managed to a timetable. With self-paced learning, the management system must be able to cope with each learner being at a different point to every other learner on a particular course.

These two key dimensions create six major types of open learning system, as shown in Figure 1.1.

Each of the six types displays particular issues for system management:

- The self-paced campus-based system offers plenty of opportunity for learner-tutor contact since both are on the same site. Learner-learner contact is equally feasible, but made problematic since different students are at different points in their courses. Assessment and tutoring have to be based around individuals rather than cohorts.
- The self-paced organization-based system is similar to the campus-based system but, in an organization, learning may be based on the learner's work and a manager rather than a tutor may be the key supporter. In other words, in an organization the natural pace may be that of the learner's work rather than that of a cohort of learners.

	Campus-based	Organization-based	Individual-based
Self-paced	Basic IT courses at the University of Lincolnshire and Humberside	National Westminster Bank CBT courses	Correspondence courses from the National Extension College
Paced	'C' computer programming at the University of Sunderland	In-company flexible learning schemes of The Open College	The Open University undergraduate programme

Figure 1.1   *Examples of the six main types of open learning system*

- The self-paced individual-based learner is the classic form of distance education. Philosophically it reflects many of the ideals of protagonists of open learning and matches theories on the nature of adult learner (eg Kolb, 1990). It is, however, fraught with organizational difficulties since learners are all at different points in their courses and tutor-student contact is generally remote.
- The paced campus-based system can be said to match the natural organizational methods of teaching institutions (terms, semesters, timetabled lecture slots) with the focus on individual responsibility for learning. The model is one of the most straightforward to manage.
- The paced organization-based system can sometimes be a poor match to an organization's needs. Organizations tend to require employee development to take place when the work needs it rather than when the employee needs it. Pacing cohorts of learners may not achieve this.
- Finally, the paced home-based system (of which the Open University is the best known example) gives supremacy to the organization's need to have all learners at the same point in their courses at the same time. It makes possible the organizational simplicity of sending out course materials to everyone at the same time, of having deadlines for assignments and set assessment dates.

Since I am taking a pragmatic view of what will count as an open learning system, a good starting point is to look at some of the case studies that I have chosen to include.

The range of systems represented in the case studies demonstrates the wide variety of educational and training operations that have open learning characteristics. Some of these are set out in Table 1.1. These range from large-scale in-company systems (eg, the National Westminster Bank) to small-scale professional schemes (eg, the Society of Cosmetic Scientists). Within the range there are systems that are largely workbook-based (eg, correspondence courses at the National Extension College), ones that make extensive use of workshops (eg, The Open College), ones with kits (eg, the Society of Cosmetic Scientists) and ones with a substantial computer-based element (eg, the National Westminster Bank). The range also includes schemes with open enrolment (eg, the National Extension College) and those were enrolment is restricted to the employees of an organization (eg, the Inland Revenue).

Table 1.1 *Some of the schemes used as examples in this book*

Example	*Type of provision*
The National Westminster Bank (a large in–company system)	**Computer-based learning (CBL)** This system delivers 125 hours of CBL throughout the UK at work locations using 300 dedicated computers. The materials on offer cover national needs. Staff can book time on these computers to suit their own patterns of working
	Self-study workbooks These are self-study materials with exercises. Staff choose which parts of the material to use and the material can be used at work or at home
	Flexible learning centres There are 11 centres, each with its own catchment area, stocked with books, videos and computer programs. The materials on offer reflect needs in that area. Staff can use the centres for advice and to borrow materials. Coaching is available from the centre staff
Society of Cosmetic Scientists (a small professional body system)	Self-study workbooks with fax support line Textbooks provided Kits provided Paced by regular assignments

Table 1.1 *Some of the schemes used as examples in this book (continued)*

Example	Type of provision
The Open College (a college which offers courses tailored to the needs of employers. Schemes can vary from small to large)	Self-study workbooks with distance tutor support and in-company line manager support – learners are part of a cohort
The National Extension College (a distance teaching college with large numbers of individual learners)	Self-study workbooks with distance tutor support – learners study as individuals
The Inland Revenue (a large-scale in-house scheme)	Self-study workbooks used by individual learners throughout the Inland Revenue

What counts as management?

Cynics sometimes ask, 'What does management do?' To some extent I have the same problem in deciding what to include under the heading 'Managing open systems'. Management can be thought of as four functions: planning, organizing, motivating and controlling (Cole, 1993, p.6). Thus tutoring is not a management function, but almost every other non-routine task which leads to successful learning has a management aspect. This book, though, concentrates on what I see as the key areas for management in open systems; these are shown in Table 1.2, together with the chapter numbers for their treatment in this book. Although in any learning system each component tends to interact with almost every other component, I have tried to make the chapters reasonably free-standing so that they can be read in any order.

I have also tried to minimize the overlap between this book and other titles in the series. In particular, readers wanting to look in more depth at the issues raised by new technology should consult *Mega-Universities and Knowledge Media* and *Using Communications Media in Open and Flexible Learning*. The problems and opportunities arising from linking open distance methods to the workplace are discussed in much greater depth in *Open and Distance Learning: Case Studies from Industry and Education*.

One could argue that the list should also include managing the production of learning materials. To do justice to that topic, another book would be needed, so I

Table 1.2 *The management areas and their chapter numbers*

2	Advising, enrolling and inducting learners
3	Providing course materials
4	Supporting learners
5	Appointing, inducting, training and monitoring tutors
6	Assessing learners
7	Monitoring and evaluating
8	Managing finance

have omitted any discussion of materials production from this book. Materials *acquisition*, though, is discussed.

I have tried to avoid writing about those generic aspects of management that apply to running any organization. For example, I do not discuss things like strategic planning or setting objectives. Nor do I talk about motivating staff or preparing budgets. In other words, I assume that the readers of this book will be competent managers wishing to apply their experience to an open system. To help them in this, I have tried to stick to what is new and different when managing an open system.

What does a system consist of?

In the context of this book, an open learning system consists of all those things which are planned for and provided by an open learning organization. These may include:

- pre-enrolment information and advice
- enrolment systems
- learning materials
- on-course information systems, eg, leaflets, brochures, online systems
- equipment, or access to equipment
- premises, eg, for tutorials
- telephone use, eg, for information or for tutorials
- tutors
- mentors
- systems to link learners, eg, self-help groups

- assessment systems
- monitoring and evaluation systems
- financial systems.

Matching systems to learner requirements

The model introduced in Figure 1.1 emphasizes that, in designing an open learning system, the two things which most affect management are:

- where your learners wish to study
- whether they will be self-paced or cohort-paced.

These are the 'where?' and 'when?' of the classic 'what?' 'when?' 'where?' and 'how?' In practice, though, a system cannot be defined by just listing what? when? where? and how? since there are constraints and opportunities which affect what is feasible and desirable. In particular, a system is a compromise between the constraints and opportunities of the learner's environment and of the subject to be studied. These factors can be systematically identified using a format such as that of Figure 1.2.

	Learner needs and expectations	Subject constraints and opportunities	Constraints and opportunities of learner's environment
Where?			
When?			
What?			
How?			

Figure 1.2 *Identifying constraints and opportunities*

When considering learner needs and expectations, all of the following might have some impact on the system design:

- Do your learners want to study with other learners?
- What type of support do they want – tutor, mentor, manager?

- Which medium do they favour? A text-based system will be very different from a computer-based or Internet-based one.
- Do your learners want access to national qualifications?
- Will they need access to equipment, eg, to computers and laboratories?

Subject constraints and opportunities include such issues as:

- Is the subject an open access subject or is access controlled (as in medicine)?
- Will you be able to offer your own award, or will you need to work with an awarding body?
- Will your learners have access to the facilities needed to learn the subject (eg, specialist equipment)?
- Can their experience be put to advantage in learning the subject?

Employment constraints and opportunities include such factors as:

- Can work achievements be recognized for course credit?
- Can what is learnt on the course be learnt *through* work?
- Will the learner be given time off for study?
- Will the learner's costs be paid by the employer?

The rest of the book

Following this brief survey of what the book is about, the remaining chapters each look at one major aspect of the management of an open system.

Chapter 2 looks at what is involved in enrolling learners, and in particular at how to manage the provision of information and guidance to prospective and new learners. In Chapter 3 I look at managing the supply of learning resources. Where might they come from? What systems are needed to get the resources from the organization to the learners and the tutors? This chapter also includes a discussion of some of the issues surrounding kits and access to practical facilities.

Supporting learners is a central activity of any open system. Chapter 4 looks at this, reviewing what a support system needs to do and who might be available to do it.

Although some open systems run without tutors, generally tutors are the main means of support. The issues of selecting, training and organizing tutors are reviewed in Chapter 5. Chapter 6 looks at assessment systems, including computer-based systems, examinations and portfolio-based assessments.

Open systems need explicit monitoring and evaluation for reasons explained in Chapter 7. This chapter looks at the difference between monitoring and evaluation, at what one might wish to monitor and evaluate, and at cost-effective methods of doing so. It is written on the assumption that the organization has no specialist research staff but nevertheless wishes to review and improve its work in a serious manner.

Chapter 8 looks at some specialist aspects of finance that are critical to running open systems. Finally, Chapter 9 provides an audit list of the main skills discussed in the book.

The book includes a large number of examples drawn from a range of systems. These are chosen to illustrate the enormous variety of effective solutions to the design of open systems. Their diversity is proof enough that there is no one right way and will, I hope, encourage readers to devise their own yet more novel solutions.

The book ends with an annotated and sectioned reading list, with titles chosen for their practical value.

Chapter 2

Managing information, guidance and enrolment

Information and advice for learners

In any learning system, learners need information and advice. Often, in class-based teaching, these needs can be met through informal and day-to-day contact. Learners can raise questions when they happen to see their tutor; tutors can use lectures and classes to make announcements. In open systems, there is less opportunity for exchanges of this type, so planning information systems becomes more important. However, some open systems (eg, campus-based schemes) may offer frequent tutor-student contact, despite the changed tutor role. This chapter has therefore to consider cases from the one extreme of correspondence courses with no student-tutor contact to the other of flexible workshops at a university where contact is regular. In discussing this range, the principle which applies is that the less the contact, the more learners' needs have to be anticipated rather than left to chance.

The information needs of tutors are looked at later in Chapter 5.

Pre-enrolment information needs

Prior to enrolment, information has to be available in order to help people decide whether they wish to enrol, and if so for which course. The sorts of things which they might need to know are set out in Table 2.1. These include issues surrounding the learner's readiness for a particular course and how well that course matches a learner's needs. A range of factors deal with issues about the process of study and the demands that will be made on the learner. Importantly, learner's also need to know what qualification (if any) the course leads to and what their opportunities and options might be after completing the course.

Few enquirers are likely to request all the information shown in Table 2.1. In some cases, enquirers need to be made aware of the questions which they have not asked. Even when this is not the case, the organization still needs to be ready to provide all this information. Ensuring that this will be so is an important management task.

Table 2.1 *Pre-enrolment information needs*

Question	*Examples of information needed*
Does the course match my needs?	• Who the course is designed for. This might be expressed in terms of staff grade for an in-company scheme (see Example 1, page 13) or educational qualifications or course prerequisites • When to take the course. For some courses, the advice might be 'any time'. For others, there might be preferred times, eg, on gaining promotion to a particular job or as preparation for a particular task
Am I ready to take the course?	• Prerequisites: the prior knowledge and skills assumed by a course
What will I learn?	• The content in terms of topics covered • The knowledge and skills that will be acquired
What will studying the course involve?	• Study time, eg, 'The total study time will be about 10 hours'

Table 2.1   *Pre-enrolment information needs (continued)*

Question	Examples of information needed
	• The types of study activity, eg, use of workbooks, computers, group work • The study periods, eg, 'You can study the course at home in your own time' or, 'You can use the computers for study between 8 am and 10 pm on Mondays to Fridays' • Where it can be studied, eg, at home, or at a centre
Over what period can I take the course?	• Start and end dates (if any) • Self- or system-paced
How will I be able to get help?	• Support system, eg, tutors, mentors, line manager support • Support methods, eg, tutorials, hot line
What will I need to provide?	• Any materials or equipment which the learner must provide
What will be provided for me?	• Any materials or equipment which the organization will provide
What will it cost?	• Course fees • Other costs, eg, exam fees, use of the learner's own telephone
Will I get a qualification?	• The qualification which can be obtained through the course • An outline of what taking the qualification involves, eg, the need to keep a portfolio, or to attend an exam centre
What will the course enable me to do next?	• Employment prospects • Access to other courses

Example 1 *An example of pre-enrolment information for courses offered by the National Westminster Bank*

Canons of Lending Course

Suitable for
Branch or unit staff, predominantly grades 7 and 6 commencing lending duties.

Recommended timing
At the same time as on-the-job training or as refresher training.

Aim of the training
To give you the core knowledge to undertake a lending role.

Content

Session DAC01 – Introduction (5 minutes)
● Brief you on the possible extent of your job responsibilities.

Session DAC02 – Principles of Lending (20 minutes)
● Outline the principles of lending.
● Explain the characteristics of unacceptable and acceptable security.

Session DAC03 – Aggregation (55 minutes)
● Apply NatWest's rules of aggregation.

Session DAC04 – Security for Lending Officers (165 minutes)
● Describe the three methods of taking security.
● Explain what security is.
● Explain why we take security.
● List the common types of security.
● State the other types of security.
● State the characteristics of good security.
● State the roles and responsibilities of security and lending staff.
● Describe the requisitioning process.

Session DAC05 – Environmental Awareness (35 minutes)
● Decide whether a business activity presents a potential environmental risk.
● Assess whether the risk is low, medium or high.
● Decide what to do to reduce the extra credit risk to NatWest because of the environmental risk.

Duration
The total study time is about 4 hours 40 minutes.
The time of individual sessions is given above.
Study should be spread over a period and each period should be no more than 3 hours.

Methods of providing pre-course information

Choosing methods for providing information and advice to potential learners involves trying to match how the learners would like to access information against what is feasible for the organization. In designing a system, questions which need to be considered include:

- How volatile is the information? If it changes frequently, it must be easy to update.
- Where will the learner be when receiving information? If potential learners will be out of reach of your staff, then the methods chosen must be ones which will work at a distance.
- Who on your staff is available to give information and advice, and how much time can they spend on it? Lengthy interviews are expensive and compete for resources that you might otherwise put into teaching.

Table 2.2 sets out some of the ways in which learners might wish to access information. Different learners, though, may prefer different methods. In general, the more forms in which information can be made available, the more likely that the needs of all potential learners will be covered.

Table 2.2   *Pre-course information access methods*

- Brochures and related materials
- Telephone discussion
- Meeting with an adviser
- Meeting current or recent learners who have taken the course
- Computerized information, eg, an interactive program (see Example 2, page 15) or the Internet
- Audio tape

Where an open learning system is employment-based, advice and information to learners can be built into other management systems for planning work and matching training needs to individual work plans. For example, many organizations have formal review or appraisal systems for their staff and these are often used to identify development needs. In the case of those organizations holding the Investors in People Award, such review systems will automatically include development needs.

Example 2 *An example of the use of a computer to provide pre-course study guidance (this extract is from the printed materials used with the computer) (University of Lincolnshire and Humberside)*

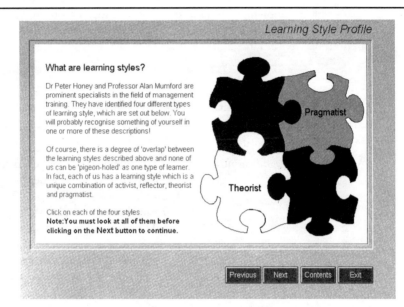

Learning Style Profile

What are learning styles?

Dr Peter Honey and Professor Alan Mumford are prominent specialists in the field of management training. They have identified four different types of learning style, which are set out below. You will probably recognise something of yourself in one or more of these descriptions!

Of course, there is a degree of 'overlap' between the learning styles described above and none of us can be 'pigeon-holed' as one type of learner. In fact, each of us has a learning style which is a unique combination of activist, reflector, theorist and pragmatist.

Click on each of the four styles.
Note: You must look at all of them before clicking on the Next button to continue.

Pragmatist

Theorist

Previous | Next | Contents | Exit

As you click on each piece of the jigsaw, you will be given a description of a different learning style. After you have read the information about all four learning styles, complete Activity 3.

Activity 3: describing the learning styles

Below is a list of twelve words or phrases. Allocate each of these to the learning style you think they describe best. You should allocate three words or phrases to each learning style.

Practical	*Outgoing*
Thoughtful	*Analytical*
Cautious	*Down-to-earth*
Enthusiastic	*Reserved*
Impulsive	*Well-informed*
No-nonsense	*Logical*

In-course information

Under this heading, I shall discuss learners' information needs which arise while taking a course, but which are not aspects of the course content. Some of these needs will be unpredictable (and open systems need to make allowance for the unpredictable) but the main area to consider is that of the predictable needs. These are summarized in Table 2.3.

Table 2.3   *Predictable in-course information needs*

Learner problem	*Examples of information needed*
What should I be doing now?	• Course timetable of fixed events, eg, tutorials, workshop sessions, assessment events (see Example 4, page 19) • For paced systems: a plan showing what should be studied in each week (or other period) • For self-paced systems: advice on preparing a personal timetable to show what will be studied when
What materials should I have?	• A list of the resources provided or needed for the course • The plans (see above) should indicate which resources are needed when
How do I get hold of or access the resources?	• An explanation of what resources will be supplied to the learner, and how • An explanation of how to access other resources, eg, how to get access to the library or how to join an Internet discussion group
How do I get study advice?	• A list of the study skills assumed by the course (see Example 5, page 20) • A list of the study skills taught on the course • Sources of help on study skills
How do I get help?	• A list of the sources of help (eg, tutor, mentor) and:

Table 2.3   *Predictable in-course information needs (continued)*

Learner problem	Examples of information needed

	– the types of problem they can help with
	  – when they are available
	  – how to access them (see Example 3, page 18, for a personalized introduction to a tutor)

How will I know how I am doing?	• Information on feedback mechanisms, eg, assignments, tutorials
What form does the assessment take?	• Details of what the assessment tasks are • When the assessment is to be done • Advice on how to do the assessment, eg, guidance on how to keep a portfolio (see Example 6, page 21)

The table includes a reference to the types of problem which learners might have on a course. The information aspects of this may prove to be the least predictable, simply because the problems are personal to each student. Here, standard information and advice systems are of little help and the learner will need to turn to a tutor, mentor or some other supporter. Tutors and other supporters need to be able to advise on a wide range of problems including:

- rearranging study around personal problems, eg, a family illness might leave a learner several weeks behind in his or her work
- providing advice on remedial work for a learner who finds he or she does not have the prerequisite knowledge and skills for the course
- supporting a learner who is finding the course difficult – the learner may feel like giving up and the supporter needs to be able to help the learner reach a decision which the learner feels is right
- supporting a learner who lacks confidence in his or her progress
- helping learners gain access to resources, eg, a line manager helping a learner to set up a work-based project which will involve other departments
- dealing with learners who are having problems in getting on with others on the course, eg, a learner who is not happy with the other members working on a group task.

You can no doubt add other problems that your learners have experienced, or that you anticipate in your open system.

Methods of providing in-course information

Once the information needs are identified, you need to decide how that information will be provided and who will be responsible for each aspect of it.

Most courses put as much information as possible into a course guide or student handbook. This is a cheap way of distributing information and has the advantage that most of what the learner needs to know is in one place. There is much anecdotal evidence, though, that learners do not read – or do not remember – what is in course guides. One solution to this is to set interactive tasks on the course guide, so getting learners to think about its contents. This works particularly well when it can be done as part of a course induction workshop.

Example 3 *A tutor biography (National Extension College)*

> John Smith studied for his history degree at Leeds University and then took a PGCE at Exeter. He worked in two secondary schools before teaching at a sixth form college as head of department. He is now an examiner for the AEB and teaches adult returners on a part-time basis. John also writes teaching materials for GCSE and some course materials for the NEC.
>
> In his spare time John enjoys cricket, swimming and walking his dogs. He and his family are interested in archaeological digs.

Post-course information

When students come to the end of courses, they often have additional information needs. For example, they may need to know about:

- how to get confirmation of their assessment result, especially if they have entered for a national qualification
- what courses they might consider doing next
- how to find out about job opportunities
- what support the organization can provide in the learner's next steps, eg, providing references.

Example 4   *A course timetable (National Police Training)*

THE TRAINERS' DEVELOPMENT PROGRAMME

This is an outline of the complete programme.

Phase One	**Selection** You have already been chosen by your force to take part in this training. You probably know by now where you will eventually be working as a trainer.	
Phase Two	**Distance Learning** A series of workbooks and the accompanying tapes. During this period you will attend a workshop when you will meet your fellow students and be introduced more fully to the Trainers' Development Programme.	This phase will last for three months.
Phase Three	**Generic Training** Held at the Training Support, Harrogate (TSH), this will give you an opportunity to check your understanding of the information in the distance learning programme, and to share your learning with others on the course. You will have the opportunity to practise and improve the skills which all the police trainers use.	This phase will last for six weeks.
Phase Four	**Workplace Briefing** At this stage you will begin to think specifically about the area of training you will be working in. You will examine the content of the courses and explore issues relevant to the course and your future role. You will be working with staff from TSH as well as staff from the training location where you will go for Phase Five of the Programme.	This phase will last for four weeks.
Phase Five	**Teaching Practice** You will be working in the training environment in which you will eventually be a trainer. With the support of a trainer development officer (TDO), you will work to develop your skills and to achieve the Police Trainer Competences.	This phase will last for two weeks.
Phase Six	**Development** Your future needs will be identified and a development plan agreed and put into action.	

Example 5   *Advice on how to study open learning materials (National Extension College)*

Making the most of your study time

Try to spend at least one hour on each study period; this gives you time to look over the notes you made in your last study period before moving on to new work. This isn't a hard and fast rule, however; some students find it just as effective to work in short bursts of 20 minutes at a time. If you do have time for a longer session, don't work for longer than three hours – you may become too tired to learn new material.

Here is the advice of one experienced NEC student:

'Don't try to do too much. Starting with five hours' study a week and building up to ten is better than starting with fifteen hours and collapsing in a heap.'

When you start work on a section of your course:

- **Read it through quickly first**
  Find out what topics you will be covering and what books or equipment you will need for the study sessions.

- **Work more slowly through the unit**
  Break it down into manageable sections, making sure you understand each point before moving on to the next.

- **Work through any self-assessment questions as you go**
  These questions will make you think back over the material you have read.

- **Make notes as you go**
  Use your own words but keep your notes brief and make sure you will be able to use them later.

- **Make your learning an *active* process**
  Don't just sit and read through the course material – you can invent further exercises to test yourself on what you've learned, or discuss what you have learned with a friend, a member of your family or another NEC student if possible.

- **Revise your work regularly**
  This will help you see your course as a whole, and not as a series of disjointed units.

If you find it difficult to study:

- **Ask your tutor for help**
  Many students do experience difficulty. Don't hesitate to seek help from your tutor.

- **Find out about NEC study skills materials**
  NEC has produced a range of courses and materials to help students to improve their study skills. More information is provided in this *Student book* in the section 'Are there other resources to help?' on pp.12–13.

Example 6   *Advice to learners on building their portfolios (National Police Training)*

HOW DO I COLLECT ACCEPTABLE EVIDENCE?

There are numerous ways of demonstrating evidence. Just looking at the competences may suggest logical sources of evidence to you. For example, to demonstrate your competence in planning learning activities, some evidence could be a lesson plan. Alternatively, to demonstrate your competence in running a lesson, your assessor may be able to observe you or you could video it. Together with your subsequent analysis of the lesson, this would provide evidence.

Do not forget, though, that one piece of evidence may not be sufficient. However, a single piece of evidence which you have recorded to show your competence in one element may also fulfil criteria for other elements. For example, your work with a group may also demonstrate your communication skills and your ability to establish a safe learning environment.

In order to present your evidence in a manageable form to the assessor, you will need to organize it using your 'Record of Achievement' folder. This includes a matrix which allows you to indicate which performance criteria relate to the various pieces of evidence you have presented. You will be given guidance to help you compile your Record of Achievement as part of your Trainer Development Programme.

The following list will give you further ideas of the kinds of evidence you could submit.

POSSIBLE SOURCES OF EVIDENCE

- Observation by another person
- Written assessment of your performance
- Self and peer assessment of your work
- Evidence of monitoring students' performance (such as a 'day book')
- Assessment centres which you have attended
- Student assessments which you have produced
- Teaching materials which you have created, adapted or used
- Lesson plans which you have written or discussed with your assessor
- Taped sessions/tutorials (audio or video)
- A tutorial (either as a trainer or as a student)
- Your action plan
- Witness evidence of an occurrence which demonstrated your competence
- Student feedback
- Performance indicators
- Reports/analysis of activities and interactions you were involved in.

Do not forget – these are just suggestions; it is up to you to provide evidence to meet the criteria given above and you may well have other ideas of how you could produce this.

Although the choice of what evidence to present is generally yours, it is suggested that any formative or summative assessments of your performance during the trainers' development programme should be included. These may be particularly useful in documenting your development as a trainer, which will be relevant to unit 3.

USING YOUR RECORD OF ACHIEVEMENT FOLDER

The Record of Achievement is your means of presenting evidence of your competence to an assessor in a manageable form. Documents which are presented as evidence may be stored in the folder itself along with the evidence sheets. The evidence sheets are for you to record written evidence or to make a note of where other evidence such as audio or video tapes can be found. You can copy and insert more evidence sheets into your folder as required. It may be possible to include a video or audio tape in a suitable holder within the folder itself.

As far as possible documentary evidence should be arranged in sequence using the page dividers to identify separate units.

As you build up your evidence sheets they can each be given a consecutive number which is then entered on the evidence matrix sheet at the front of the folder. You may divide your Record of Achievement into more than one folder if you find this more convenient.

Methods of providing post-course information

In systems where the learner will stay with the organization after completing a course (eg, a university student who has finished one module and moves on to another, or a learner taking an on-the-job course) providing post-course information is not particularly difficult. There will, after all, be systems within such organizations for guiding learners. For example, in a university there will be personal tutors who can help in module choice and careers staff who can help in career choice. In workplaces, learners will have line managers who can either advise on next steps, or point the learner to more specialist advice within the organization.

Where the learner is not part of the organization which provides the course, post-course information is more problematic – indeed so problematic that many providers make no arrangements for it. The difficulty usually stems from the fact that, while taking a course, the learner's main contact (and sometimes sole contact) is his or her tutor. Once the course is completed, the tutor ceases to have responsibility for the learner – such tutors are rarely paid to give post-course advice. The learner, though, may not have built up a rapport with any other person in the organization and so is uncertain about who to contact.

There are various solutions to this problem. Some organizations contract their tutors (or other support staff) to provide support after the learners have completed their courses. Others use central support staff to respond to ex-students' needs.

Enrolment systems

In some organizations the term 'enrolment' may include providing information and advice. In this section, though, I look only at what happens after that advice has been given.

On several occasions when I have enrolled on an adult education course, the enrolment mêlée has left me incredulous. It usually consists of a vast number of queues (for what is often unclear) at the head of which two things happen: you give your name and hand over a fee. You are enrolled. With whom, for what, with what end and so on are left unstated.

Enrolment systems for open learning need to be much more sophisticated than this. In this section I will look at why that is so and how systems can be designed to meet the needs of the learner and the organization.

The purpose of an enrolment system in most organizations is fourfold:

● To create a contract between the organization and the learner, making the terms clear to the learner and obtaining the learner's agreement to them. (If the scheme is in-house and does not involve the learner paying fees, the 'contract' will refer to the commitment that each party is making, rather than a legal obligation.)
● To collect the information that the organization requires to meet the learner's needs. A decision has to be made as to which items of information should be collected on enrolment and which later. For example, some systems collect on enrolment all the information that the central administration needs, leaving tutors to collect later information that only they need.
● To provide learners with the information that they need between the time of enrolment and starting the course
● To collect information needed for management and funding purposes.

How these requirements can be broadly met is set out in Table 2.4. This table distinguishes in sections 1 and 2 between the need to create a contractual relationship in fee-paying systems and the need to have an agreement in non-fee paying systems. Section 3 of the table deals with information collecting (meeting the needs of the organization) and information giving (meeting the needs of newly enrolled students).

Table 2.4   *Functions of an enrolment system*

Enrolment purpose	Examples of action needed
1. Fee-paying systems To create a contract between the organization and the learner (See Example 7, page 26, where the contractual aspects of the form can be clearly seen.)	• Written terms of the contract, including the fees to be paid by the learner and when they they are due • learner's signature to show acceptance of the terms • the signature of any other party to the agreement, eg, the learner's sponsor
2. Non-fee paying systems To create a commitment between the organization and the learner	• written terms of the agreement, including the commitment expected of both parties • learner's signature to show acceptance of the terms • the signature of any other party to the agreement, eg, the learner's line manager
3. All systems To collect the information that the organization requires to meet the learner's needs (Example 7, page 26, shows one way of collecting this type of data.)	This will vary with the organization, but might include: • personal and demographic details • contact addresses and telephone numbers (eg, work and home) • courses to be taken • educational history – if needed, eg, for giving advice or providing exemptions from certain courses • proposed study schedule – unless fixed by the organization • details of any sponsors or supporters (eg, line manager's details)

Table 2.4   *Functions of an enrolment system (continued)*

Enrolment purpose	Examples of action needed
To provide learners with the information that they need between enrolment and starting the course	Again, this will vary with the organization, but might include: • the course timetable – or, if self-paced, a format for the learners to make their own • advice on preparing for the course – eg, materials to gather or contacts to make for project work • details of what course materials will arrive (or need to be collected) and when • tutor (or other key supporter) details, including how to contact them • a contact point for any outstanding queries

Example 7 *An example of an enrolment form for a distance learning course (National Extension College)*

CONFIDENTIAL

National Extension College
18 Brooklands Avenue
Cambridge CB2 2HN
United Kingdom
Tel: 01223 316644 Fax: 01223 313586
Vat No: 215 7137 79 Reg No: 292829

NEC
NATIONAL
EXTENSION
COLLEGE

For office use only
Student number: SS   Tutor number: T

Enrolment form

Name and address

YOUR NAME AND ADDRESS (IN CAPITALS)
(Not needed if correctly entered above)

Name   Title

Address

                                  Postcode

Tel: (evening)   Tel: (day)

Date of birth   Female ☐   Male ☐

If you are normally out in the day and can give an alternative name and address for signed receipt of a parcel of course materials, please indicate here, for example a neighbour or your business address

Name

Address

                                  Postcode

Your choice of courses

Course title	Course code	Exam date if applicable	Course fee
e.g. *Maths GCSE Intermediate*	*GC26*	*Summer 96*	*£220*
Less discount, if applicable – see Fees List			
Less tax relief, if applicable (I attach form VTR1)			
Add the cost of overseas postage, if applicable (10% of the course fee for EU countries; 15% for the rest of the world)			
		Total	

Method of payment

Select any of the following 5 methods of payment.

Payment in full

☐ **1.** I enclose a cheque/postal order/PO Giro for £_____ made payable to the **National Extension College Trust Limited** for the full cash fee.

☐ **2.** Please charge my ☐ Access/Mastercard ☐ Visa/Barclaycard ☐ American Express ☐ Diners Club ☐ Switch card with the full cash fee *(tick as appropriate)*.

Card Number

Expiry Date   Issue number (Switch cards only) ☐

Address known to credit card company if different from the one shown on this form

                                  Postcode

Signature (I am over 18 years old)   Date

☐ **3.** Please invoice my employer/sponsor for the full course fee (UK only). I enclose an official order form from my employer/sponsor confirming this arrangement. (We can only accept an invoiced enrolment if it is accompanied by an official order or letter.)

Employer's name

Address

                                  Postcode

Tel: Contact name

Payment by instalment

Check your deposit and instalments on the Fees List. You must send the deposit with this Enrolment Form. If you need any help in calculating your instalments, contact our **Accounts Department** on **01223 450209**.

☐ **4.** I enclose £_____ deposit and undertake to pay the balance by_____ consecutive monthly payments of £_____
Please remember to complete the Bankers Standing Order Form included in the **How to Pay for Your Course** leaflet if you select this method of payment, and attach it to your Enrolment Form.
Giro: We also accept payment by PO Giro – our Giro number is 278 3258. If you wish to pay by Giro Standing Order, you can obtain this form from your Post Office.

☐ **5.** Please charge my ☐ Access/Mastercard ☐ Visa/Barclaycard ☐ American Express ☐ Diners Club ☐ Switch card *(tick as appropriate)* with the sum of £_____ in respect of my deposit immediately upon receipt of this enrolment and thereafter _____ consecutive monthly payments of £_____
Fill in the credit card form in Section 2 above if you select this method of payment.

Please sign

I wish to enrol as a student for the course(s) shown. I agree to pay the fees as stated and be bound by the **Conditions of enrolment** printed overleaf.

Signed   Date

If you are under 18, please ask your parent or guardian to sign this statement.

I hereby accept responsibility for the total fee above

                              Father/Mother/Guardian

PLEASE ALSO COMPLETE THE DETAILS OVERLEAF

17a

More information about you

The questions which follow are optional. They will help us advise you on your studies, but if you decide not to answer any of them it will not affect your enrolment in any way. Your responses will be treated in the strictest confidence.

Occupation: what is your current (or most recent) occupation?

Have you studied with NEC before? ☐ Yes ☐ No If yes, please give your old student number, if you know it, and approximate date

Number: Date:

Please list the qualifications you have and the date obtained

Do you have access to any of the following equipment at home to help with your studies?
☐ video recorder   ☐ fax   ☐ e-mail
☐ computer   ☐ CD–ROM   ☐ internet

Are there any courses you would be interested in studying in the future?

Our policy is to try to help students with difficulties or special circumstances where we can. Please indicate below if you have a disability, or anything else you would like us to know about.

How did you find out about NEC?

(This information will help us to inform more people about NEC courses)

1. Advertisement *(please state publication & date)*

2. Professional institution *(please state which one)*

3. Company recommendation

4. Friend/relative

5. Other *(please state)*

What newspapers do you read on a regular basis?

What journals or magazines do you read on a regular basis?

If you would like us to send a free copy of our *Guide to Courses* to friends or colleagues who may wish to study with NEC, please complete their details below.

Name

Address

Postcode

Conditions of enrolment

Please read these conditions of enrolment in full before sending your enrolment form. They do not affect your statutory rights in any way. If you are enrolling for our University of London, Institute of Linguists or Engineering Council tuition service, please phone our Degree and Professional Service on **01223 450231** for a separate enrolment form.

1 Your course and tuition fees
● For all courses developed by NEC, your course fee covers the cost of your course materials, together with tuition for up to three years from the date of your enrolment, as long as the syllabus you enrolled on remains available for this time.
● Your course fee does not include the cost of any additional books you need to purchase, or the cost of registration or examination fees to awarding bodies.
● NEC cannot accept responsibility for changes to the availability or syllabus content of any exams run by other organisations.
● The offer of free tuition if you fail your exams is conditional on the syllabus you enrolled for still being examined.

2 Paying for your course
● Your course fees are payable in full when you enrol, or you can pay by instalment for any course costing **£99 or over**. The instalments for each course are set out in the appropriate NEC **Fees list**. You must enclose your instalment deposit when you enrol.
● NEC welcomes enrolments from overseas students, but we do have to make an additional charge to cover postage. Please add 10% to your course fee if you are an EU resident, or 15% if you live outside Europe. If you pay by instalment, please add this charge to your deposit.

3 Special discounts
● If you are a pensioner, on income support or unemployment benefit, you are entitled to 15% off the course fee for any NEC course costing **£99 or over**, providing you send supporting evidence with your enrolment.
● If you are a former NEC student (and quote your student number), you are entitled to 10% off the course fee for any NEC course costing **£99 or over**. This offer cannot be used in conjunction with the supported income discount above.

4 Cancelling your course
● If within 30 days from the despatch of your enrolment, you decide that the course you have chosen is unsuitable, you have a choice of:
course transfer: if you choose to transfer to another NEC course, NEC will retain 25% of the **full course fee** to cover administrative costs, plus a charge for each assignment marked by your tutor. The balance will be put towards the fee for your new course
course cancellation: if you wish to cancel your course and receive a cash refund, a cancellation fee will be deducted based on 40% of the **full course fee**, plus a charge for each assignment marked.
● We regret that it is not possible to change or cancel any course costing **under £99**.
● If you cancel your course after 30 days, a cancellation fee will be deducted based on 40% of the **full course fee**, plus a charge for each assignment marked by your tutor. The balance can only be used as a transfer right towards another NEC course, and will not be refunded as cash. All transfer rights must be used **within six months** from the date of your cancellation.
● NEC cannot accept any requests for cancellation **later than six months** from the date of your enrolment.
Please note: the full course fee means the fee as stated in the *Guide to Courses* or related NEC literature, and does not include any special discount or offer made by NEC in the *Guide* or at any other time.

Enrolment checklist

Have you:
☐ checked your name, address and postcode are correct?
☐ filled in the right course codes and fees?
☐ chosen your method of payment and enclosed a cheque, credit card or Banker's Standing Order Form as appropriate?
☐ attached supporting documents if you are claiming a discount, or form **VTR1** if you are claiming tax relief?
☐ read the **Conditions of enrolment** and signed this form? (Your enrolment is not valid unless you have done so.)
If you have any problems filling in this form, please phone NEC's Customer Services Department on **01223 316644**.

Send this enrolment form to us, using the reply paid label.

If you are paying by credit card, you can fax your enrolment direct to NEC on **01223 313586** or phone us on **01223 316644**. Please make sure you quote your credit card number.
We will process your enrolment immediately.

The National Extension College
18 Brooklands Avenue
Cambridge CB2 2HN
United Kingdom

NEC
NATIONAL
EXTENSION
COLLEGE

176

Chapter 3

Managing learning resources

Managing the provision of materials

This book does not deal with the development of learning materials, nor with the management of the materials development process. So, in this chapter, I assume that the materials that your learners need exist somewhere and that you are faced with the problem of how to make sure that the right materials get to the right learners at the right time. Readers wishing to look in more depth at the development of materials should consult other titles such as *Preparing Materials for Open, Distance and Flexible Learning* and *Teaching Through Self-instruction* (see 'Materials development' in the further reading section).

Acquisition

If you are manufacturing your own materials (eg, printing workbooks or copying discs) then this section will not apply to your system. If, however, you will obtain your materials from another supplier, you need to consider the following points. The key questions to ask are:

- Do the materials meet the learners' needs?
- During the period that we intend to use them, will the materials be available *unchanged*?

- Will the price remain unchanged?
- If the supplier should at any point be unable to supply us, would we have the right to make copies to meet our learners' needs?
- What plans does the supplier have to revise or discontinue the materials?
- Do we have a legally binding agreement with the supplier?

While the first bullet is self-explanatory, the others may seem pedantic. However, the points all reflect problems that have arisen in the running of various open systems.

Acquisition is problematic because, once you have chosen to use certain materials, you will need to build other parts of your system around them. For example, one organization wrote a set of study guides around the materials produced by another organization. Having completed the study guides, the first organization then found that the second had revised all the learning materials. This necessitated a huge rewrite of the study guides.

Another common problem is titles going out of print and the supplier being unable or unwilling to produce more copies. Of course, you can always choose to buy enough copies in advance of enrolment, but (a) you may not know how many copies you need and (b) you may not have the resources to fund such a purchase.

The final problem to consider is that of the supplier revising the materials. While the revised materials may be 'better' than the previous ones, they may not be better for you since you may have to revise your own programme (eg, produce new assessments) before you can use the new materials. If the materials are computer-based, then the new version may even require an updated operating system or more memory.

All these problems point to the necessity for you to consider worst cases when planning your scheme and to have a clear written agreement as to what the supplier guarantees to do for you, at what price and over what period.

Identification of materials

It may be that on some occasion a student has attended the wrong set of lectures at university. It is certainly the case that some students in open systems have studied the wrong open learning materials and turned up at an examination only to find the questions did not match what they had studied. This emphasizes the importance in open systems of watertight methods of identifying learning materials – methods that will work when learner, tutor and administrative centre are all in different places.

Systems for identifying course materials usually start by separating the idea of a course from the various and distinct items (sometimes called 'components') of material used to make up that course. In other words:

- each item of course material (a workbook, a study guide, a disc) has its own identifier
- a course is treated as a collection of separate items.

The question of how to identify the components then arises. Whatever the system, it must, for any one component, be able to locate:

- the unique title
- the edition, eg, '2nd edition', 'version 3', '1996 exams edition'.

Since titles tend not to be unique (how many works share the title 'An introduction to statistics'?), components are often given a code – something which can be unique.

An example of a component coding system is shown in Figure 3.1. Here a computer disc called *Cost of living spreadsheets* has been given the unique code D012 (D for disc) and the edition is the 1996 one. The edition date could be incorporated into the code as D012/1996 if necessary.

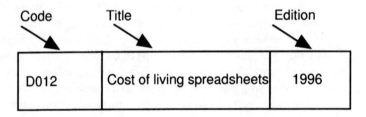

Figure 3.1   *A component coding system*

Once a component coding system is in place, courses can be made up by listing the required components. Table 3.1 is an example of a list of components for a 'Statistics in economics' course.

Table 3.1   *A course made up from components*

Item	Title	Edition
W261	*Statistics in economics* (workbook)	3rd edition
D012	*Cost of living spreadsheets* (disc)	1996 edition
AB034	*Statistics in economics assignments*	1996 edition

Storage

All except the smallest systems tend to have two storage systems: a day-to-day despatch system and a long-term bulk system.

The day-to-day dispatch system normally has course materials made up into ready-for-use packs for each course. The long-term storage system usually keeps each component separately from the others. There are two reasons for this:

- when stored as delivered from reproduction, components generally take up less space than when made up into courses
- making up components into courses uses costly labour, so is not done until necessary.

Dispatch

The first thing to consider in a dispatch system is what will trigger the initial dispatch. Various triggers can be used:

- the enrolment system can be designed to generate a dispatch request
- the request may have to come from the learner's tutor. For example, in systems where the course starts with an induction session, the tutor normally orders the materials to hand out to the learners
- where a cohort of learners is going through a course, dispatch may be triggered by a date, eg, course XYZ to go to cohort ABC on 1 September 1996
- in some systems (especially in-company schemes), the learners may have to go to a centre in order to collect their materials.

Later dispatches may then follow a timetable or be triggered by further events such as:

- the tutor requesting that materials be sent to certain learners
- the learner requesting the materials
- the completion of a particular stage of a course, eg, a particular assignment.

Whatever the trigger, the system needs to have a method of recording what was sent and when. This is where the component and course identification systems become useful. The system can be used to record the dispatch of:

- a total course, eg, 'course XYZ v2 sent' – recording which version of a course has been issued effectively records which components and which versions of those components have been issued
- a part course, eg, 'course XYZ v2 part 1' – again the particular components and their versions are known from this code
- particular components, eg, 'disc D012 v3' sent.

Stock control

Stock control systems have three main functions:

(a)   to show how much stock has been used in the year to date, for what purpose and the value used

(b)   to show the current stock level and its value

(c)   to forecast stock requirements and record current orders.

The detail of how this can be done is suggested in Table 3.2. Clearly, just how detailed a system needs to be depends on its size and complexity. A scheme with just a few items of learning materials (or all its materials on a central computer server) needs a minimal stock control function. A scheme with many components and many suppliers needs a sophisticated system to make sure that titles do not go out of stock and also to keep costs under control.

An important aspect of stock control is stock valuation. In any system which is subject to audit, the auditors must approve the stock valuation system. Where there is no audit requirement, it is advisable to consult an accountant or finance officer over the stock valuation method in order to protect oneself from later accusations of faulty accounting. (The basic issue here is at what value to record the various copies: the price paid for them? What they are worth now? What it would cost to buy more today? In some cases, stock may exist but have no value, as in the case of out-of-date materials that can no longer be issued to learners.)

The revision file

Users of materials quickly find all those misprints that somehow got through the production system. They also often make suggestions for improvements. Any system for controlling materials therefore needs a method for recording these comments so that they can be considered later by editorial staff. At a minimum such a system needs to record:

- the comment or correction
- the component to which it refers, with the component version
- the location of the problem, eg, the page number.

These comments need to be kept in a form in which they can be reviewed by editorial staff so that they can decide which comments need:

- immediate action, eg, a serious error which needs an immediate erratum sheet
- action when the next manufacture run takes place
- action when the next revision takes place
- no action.

Table 3.2 *Stock system functions*

Main stock control function	Examples of detailed aspects
To show how much stock has been used in the year to date, for what purpose and the value used.	• Record how many copies have been used for what purpose. Typically, a system might record stock issues as: – learner use – tutor and other organizational use – marketing use • Record the value of the stock consumed, using the valuation system approved by the organization's accountants
To show the current stock level and its value	• Record the physical copies in stock • Record the value of the current stock, using the valuation system approved by the organization's accountants
To forecast stock requirements and record current orders	• Record the number of physical copies in stock which are reserved for known commitments, eg, if 100 learners have enrolled, but still need to be sent materials, then the stock system needs to show that 100 copies are reserved stock • Forecast how many additional copies will be needed (excluding those on order) within the manufacture period, ie, if it takes six weeks to get further copies of an item, then, at any one time, enough copies for the next six weeks' use need to be in stock

Fred Lockwood has described these three types of action as first aid, surgery and post-mortem.

Pending such central action having been taken, tutors will often have to do something themselves. This may involve warning their students of errors and omissions, providing their students with temporary erratum sheets, and producing additional materials to cover serious gaps.

In some systems (eg, the National Westminster Bank) the central unit provides a service to other parts of the organization. In these cases, the decision to amend or revise a course lies with the sponsor rather than with the central unit.

Managing Internet-based materials

The advent of the Internet offers a method of simultaneously storing and dispatching learning materials. Once the materials are loaded on to the Internet, learners can access them at any time and at any place in the world.

Some materials on the Internet give the appearance of lectures notes which have been put on the Internet with little or no alteration. In other cases, what is on the Internet is essentially a course guide, ie most of the learning material is offline in the form of books, journals and so on.

Materials can be designed for being studied on screen (expensive in terms of telephone time) or for being down-loaded on to the learner's hard disc for later study. Example 8 shows some course text that could be partly studied on screen, or could be downloaded. In this case, since reference is made to a textbook, part of the study has to be offline. An interesting variant on online delivery of materials is to use the Internet to help learners find their own materials. Students on this geography Internet course at the University of Colorado can click a button which takes them to a prepared page of key resources in Australia (Example 9).

Internet-shaped courses

Examples 8 and 9 are recognizably traditional university courses being delivered using a new medium. The use of the Internet does not seem to have influenced the content and teaching style. A development at the University of Sunderland suggests that the Internet does require us to rethink how we teach. I shall illustrate this through the University's work on a course called 'Poetica', although some of the lessons have been learnt more broadly from other Internet courses being developed at Sunderland.

Poetica is a course in the metrical analysis of poetry. It is on the Internet at http://www.sund.ac.uk/~us0cma/poetica.html and offers students two weeks of independent study as part of a one-semester module. The course includes a number of features:

- online study texts in HTML (hypertext mark-up language)
- formative assessment exercises to help students check their progress
- a moderated notice board to keep students up to date with new developments on the course

Example 8 *An example of learning materials on the Internet. These can be studied on-
or offline (University of Colorado)*

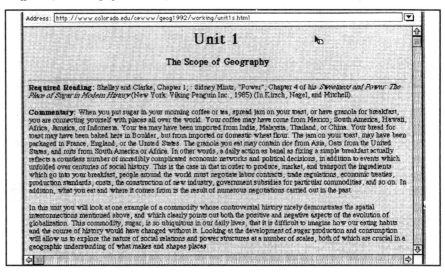

Example 9 *A course Internet site which provides access to other Internet learning resources
(University of Colorado)*

- a moderated electronic conference; tutors can examine this to identify common problems, just as they would in the classroom
- electronic mail for student–tutor communication.

An overview of what Poetica offers can be seen in Examples 10 and 11.

Example 10   *Part of the Poetica home page (University of Sunderland)*

POETICA

Pour la version française appuyez <u>ici, s.v.p.</u> Für die deustche Version <u>SOCRATES</u> - a call for institutions across Europe

Programme for Orientation, Education and Telematics Implementation in Critical Analysis.
POETICA uses hypertext structures to integrate electronic digital course material into the teaching and learning of poetry and stylistic analysis of poetry. It is part of the English Studies Degree Programme at the University of Sunderland in the module ELL 104 Stylistic Analysis, a 20-credit, level 1 course. POETICA also uses hypertext structures to provide telematic access to contemporary poetry.

Electronic Courseware - The On-line Study Texts

- <u>Annotation of Stress</u>
- <u>Introduction to Metre</u>
- <u>Aims and the Poet</u>
- <u>Stress - Historical Theories</u>
- <u>Control and Conformity in Verse</u>

Example 11   *More of the Poetica home page (University of Sunderland)*

Telematic Participation

- <u>Assessment</u>
- <u>Poetica Answer-Garden</u>

Sample Assignments

- <u>SA1 Examination Question</u>
- <u>SA2 Deixis in Verse</u>

POETICA ~ NOTICEBOARD

Examination Question: The specimen examination question for ELL104, focussing on close reading of poetry, is now available under SA1 above. This will form the basis of an electronic newsgroup conference here in POETICA.

Surgeries: If you still feel in need of some help with POETICA, please e-mail Charlie Mansfield, or post a message in the Newsgroup local.poetica. We can then set up some extra help sessions

E-Mail News:- Nearly every student in English Studies has now applied for an e-mail number. Your numbers are with Richard Terry in Forster for collection.

From the management viewpoint, the importance of Poetica is the lessons that have been learnt about running courses on the Internet. Poetica has shown that merely putting lecture-type text on the Internet is not a productive way to use its possibilities. Rather, what the Internet offers is a chance to guide learners through new material by taking advantage of the layered nature of hypertext. In the case of Poetica, the layers chosen were the administrative text level, the study texts and the source texts. This structure is shown in Example 12. In one sense, this process of guiding learners through layers is a function of any good teaching; however, in the case of Internet courses, it perhaps becomes more critical to get this right. Experience with the first version of Poetica showed that learners easily felt lost in a mass of Internet pages. The layering, together with a reorganization of the home page, provides learners with the guidance they need to overcome this feeling.

Example 12   *The layered structure of a hypertext course (Mansfield and Robertson, 1996)*

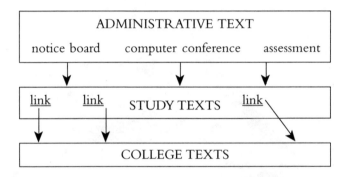

Further examination of the effects of the hypertext structure on the teaching process has suggested that:

- such courses can be used to equip learners with tools for problem-solving and data analysis
- the layering structure can be used to help students learn to quarry texts (or other data) in order to solve problems
- this approach to study can help learners find new connections between different items of information which they might not have found in a linear text
- printed texts may still be needed. In the case of Poetica, a booklet entitled *Writing on Wires* was written to teach learners how to use the Internet.

The experience has suggested that, to be successful, an Internet course needs:

- a clear setting of parameters by the lecturer – this gives value to the course
- a guidebook that takes the learner through the study activities – this can be Internet- or print-based
- clear outcomes which are given value either through being assessed, or through creating electronic materials which learners can use later in their work.

This relationship between the three ingredients for success has been summarized in Example 13.

Example 13   *A model for Internet course design (Mansfield and Robertson, 1996)*

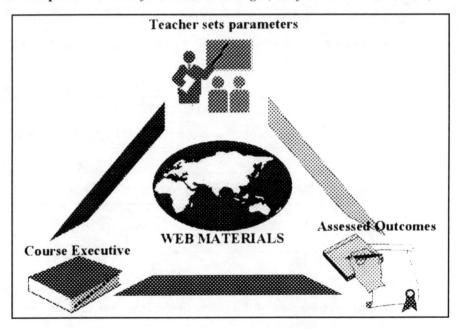

In summary, then, the Poetica experience suggests two critical lessons for managers of open systems wishing to use the Internet for course delivery. First, putting a course onto the Internet should not be the mere delivery of lecture notes. An Internet course is an entity in its own right and its development requires deep thinking by academic staff and appropriate time and resources. Second, management will have to provide extensive staff development opportunities if staff are to develop the understanding and skills needed for effective use of the Internet.

Managing the provision of equipment

The expense of equipment means that few schemes provide it to learners. Instead, providers may try:

- avoiding the need for equipment altogether
- helping the learners gain access to someone else's equipment.

Some organizations do provide kits for practical subjects. For example, the Society of Cosmetic Scientists supplies kits such as the one shown in Example 14. If you have to provide equipment the following points will need to be considered.

Example 14   *An example of a distance learning kit (Society of Cosmetic Scientists)*

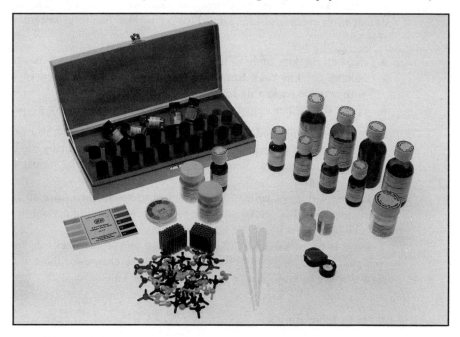

Providing kits

The first thing to consider once you are sure that the kit meets the course requirements is whether the kit is safe for use by learners. Here, you have the problem that what might be considered safe in a supervised laboratory may not be safe when used by a lone learner. You will therefore need to seek advice from an expert in the area over:

- What are the risks when using the equipment?
- What advice to learners is needed to minimize the risks? (See Example 15 for part of the safety advice which accompanies one kit.)

The safety aspects of kits and of the instructions for their use need careful consideration. Some aspects of the COSHH (Control of Substances Hazardous to Health) legislation apply to the distribution of kits. This legislation is primarily concerned with the protection of employees, but aspects of it stretch to 'other persons'. This could include home-based and other students. In particular, the COSHH regulations clearly state that a risk assessment is needed for all persons (employees, students and others such as their families). Such an assessment has to be carried out 'so far as is reasonably practicable' (HSE, 1996, pp.4–5).

Kits can be included in a course fee, sold separately, or rented to learners. Generally kits are both expensive and reusable so the main issues are ones of dispatch, recovery and checking. That is, any kit handling system needs to be able to:

- dispatch the kits safely to learners
- receive the kits back from learners – ie, the learners need to be provided with suitable packaging for the return of the kit
- check the kit before reissue – this is generally an expensive process.

Both journeys will need insurance to cover damage in transit. You may also wish to charge students for insurance against accidental damage during use by the them. Generally, organizations charge a deposit, refundable on the return of the kit in good condition.

The regulations of your carrier will need to be checked since all carriers place restrictions on what can be sent. They may permit sending certain items but only if packed in particular ways.

Some parts of kits may have to regarded as consumables, eg, chemicals and batteries. In this case, you will need to be able to charge for these and to make it clear that they should not be returned with the kit.

Providing access to laboratories

Some courses need access to laboratories. The main options to consider are:

- learner access to a laboratory at his or her place of work
- learner access to a laboratory being used by other learners
- residential or weekend schools or other systems for the block hire of laboratory time.

Example 15   *A part of the safety advice for a kit on a distance learning course (Society of Cosmetic Scientists)*

---

5. SAFETY
The practical work described in the accompanying perfumery module can be carried out in safety if you follow instructions carefully. However, smelling perfumes may produce reactions in someone with an asthmatic condition or sensitive bronchial tubes. It is advisable therefore to take shallow 'sniffs'. Avoid inhaling deeply.

5.1 A Guide to Safe Working
This is an opportunity to reinforce comments in the module about where to carry out the activities and what surface to leave the sample sticks on, supported in the bulldog clips or pegs.

The ideal room for these activities should neither be too hot nor too cold. A study at home or personal office at work or spare bedroom should be fine. However, you may experience difficulty if you work in a room where there are other odours. So avoid newly painted or recently polished areas. Rooms frequented by smokers or where there are food or other domestic odours lingering may also make the activities more difficult to complete successfully.

It is good practice when you know you are to 'smell' solutions to refrain from the use of personal fragrances (cologne, perfume or after-shave). You will be required to 'smell' strips that have been left overnight and careful thought should be given as to where to leave them. They should not be kept in an area where they may pick up other odours and they should not be left on polished wood or plastic surfaces, as the perfume material may affect the finish. Needless to say, they should be kept out of reach of children and animals. Let others who may use the area you choose know what you are doing. You will need to work with a partner in some activities. Let your partner know of any hazards involved.

Working with small quantities is an important safety factor but you or others may still come into contact with the perfumery substances. It is prudent to anticipate such contact and, because some may be more adversely affected than others, to prepare in advance. You should read through the first aid section before beginning experiments and have readily to hand:

● a supply of absorbent paper – paper towel or paper handkerchief or other – for mopping up spills;
● a glass of clean drinking water, kept covered, in case of splashes to mouth or accidental ingestion.

Always wash any gloves you wear, and your hands, after working with chemicals.

6.   CHEMICAL SPILLAGES
The small amounts used hardly warrant a specialist section on this topic. The nature of the oils used is such as to cause few worries. However, as mentioned earlier, the liquids may affect polished wood or plastic surfaces so if you have to work on such an area it may be as well to protect it with a material or paper which lies flat to provide a smooth working surface. Any other areas affected can be wiped free of spilled substances using absorbent paper. The paper should be deposited in a bin.

Contact with skin, eyes or clothing, or if you breathe vapours in, or swallow any substance as the result of spillage, should be dealt with according to the coded first aid instructions on the Safety Information Card which should always be kept at hand.

In each case, learners will need to be provided with a detailed work programme, eg, a set of experiments to carry out. However, the more problematic issue is that of supervision. Owners of laboratories wish to be assured that learners will not harm themselves, the laboratory or other users. In practice this usually means that open learning students can only gain access to laboratories in which someone is formally prepared to act as supervisor. When that happens, the supervisor will need briefing on:

- the learning outcomes that the learner is expected to achieve
- the programme of work which the learner is to carry out
- any special activities that the supervisor should conduct, eg, assessment.

Providing access to computers

Many learners choose to use computers in their studies, for example to word-process assessments, but in this section I am only concerned with the issues that arise when computer use is a requirement of the course. This might be to:

- access the learning materials
- communicate with tutors and other learners
- run interactive learning software
- use standard programs (eg, word-processing or a spreadsheet) to process course data
- write programs
- create databases
- access remote databases.

In work-based schemes, the first thing to consider is whether the workplace computers can be used for the course. This may be impracticable during normal working hours. Even if the computers are free outside those hours, the learners may not be willing to study then.

Where the existing workplace computers cannot be used, additional learning resource computers are sometimes installed; in other cases, employers may create open learning centres with a wide range of resources, including computers.

What, then are the issues if work computers cannot be used?

First, you need to find out whether most or all of your learners have private access to computers and, if so, to which models. Some groups of learners (eg, managers and professionals) may be well supplied with computers; others (eg, unemployed people on basic skills courses) are very unlikely to have access to suitable computers.

Where learners are using their own computers, it is likely that different learners will have different types of computer, each needing its own software. This creates problems when the centre intends to distribute software. The problems which can arise from the variety of hardware in use by students are discussed in Jones *et al.* (1992). They conclude (p.122):

'These various incidents highlight the fact that for home-based computing, the lack of standardisation remains an issue, even when ostensibly 'compatible' equipment is being used. Supporting a variety of equipment is difficult for any institution.'

Where students are using their own computers, learners may need help and advice. This is not easy to provide at a distance. Various methods have been tried to help learners set up their computer systems including those listed in Table 3.3.

Table 3.3 *Methods of helping learners set up their computers (based on Jones* et al. *1992, pp. 122–3)*

Method	Reported problems
Written guides	Novices find it difficult to diagnose the nature of their problem
Computer induction meetings	Low attendance
Using the first tutorial to resolve computer problems	Those attending can range from total novices to experienced users. Tutors find this range difficult to handle

Some learning tasks do not require a specific make of software. For example, learners can learn to word-process using any package; learners can create and interpret spreadsheets using a wide range of applications; and learners can use e-mail systems and the Internet when using one of many browsers or communications packages. In other words, designing learning tasks that do not require a specific make of software or a specific operating system is a good way to avoid many of the problems. (The advent of the Java computer language will help here. The Java language can be used to create programs that will run on a wide range of computers. All the user needs is a 'Java reader' for his or her computer. It is likely that leading computer manufacturers will include Java readers as standard with their machines in the near future.)

When the learning outcomes can only be achieved using a specific piece of software, access to suitable computers is likely to become a problem. For longer courses, computer rental can be considered. For short courses, the only solution may be for learners to travel to selected locations to use the specified equipment.

Learners' attitudes to computers will affect their willingness to use the equipment and the level of training and support that they need. Learners may find computer conferencing impersonal and find that they rarely make contributions; video conferencing may be seen as intimidating (Mason, 1994). These and other problems emphasize the need for developing learner support and tutor training systems alongside the introduction of computers into course delivery and assessment. Merely putting a course online (which has an apparent air of ease of access) will not ensure successful use.

Using telephones

The telephone is one of the most widely available pieces of equipment that can be used in open learning. Its main role is in learner support although, as fax, it can be used to distribute learning materials (see Example 16, page 47). Bates (1995) has summarized the range of uses of the telephone in distance education, shown in Table 3.4.

Almost all open systems involve learners studying mostly at times and locations when their supporters are not present. The learner may, at most times, be isolated

Table 3.4 *Purposes and modes of organization for telephone use in distance education (Bates, 1995, p. 166)*

	Purpose and frequency		
Organizational mode	*Direct teaching*	*Tutoring/counselling*	*Administration*
1 One-to-one	Rarely	Frequently	Frequently between individual staff
2 Tutor with one remote group	Occasionally, especially on split campuses	Rarely	Rarely
3 Audio-conferencing	Rarely	Frequently, particularly when students are too scattered to meet face-to-face	Frequently for meetings to bring in remote staff
4 Tutor with several remote groups	Frequently at Wisconsin	Rarely	Occasionally, between groups of staff at different campuses

from other learners. The telephone can be used to link learner and tutor, learners and tutor or learner and learner when they are physically separated. Given that this chapter is on the management of resources, the detailed aspects of the use of the telephone in open learning will be left until later. Here, the resource management aspects will be looked at.

Any open system needs to have clear guidelines as to what types of telephone communication are encouraged and how such communication should be initiated. Table 3.5 sets out some of the key issues for resource management. You can see from this that the main management issues are:

- being clear about what telephones will be used for
- briefing learners, tutors and staff about those uses
- being clear about who pays for the calls.

The table does not include encouraging learners to telephone each other. If you do wish to encourage that, then you need to decide how learners will access each others' telephone numbers. Will you circulate them? (This would need the prior permission of the learners. Such permission could be sought at the point of enrolment.) Or will you leave the learners to work out a system for themselves? The costs of using the telephone in open systems are fully discussed in Chapter 8 of Bates (1995).

Providing access to computer conferencing

Like telephones, computer conferencing can be used for many purposes, including the delivery of teaching. There are three basic ways in which an organization might provide access to computer conferencing:

- companies offering work-based schemes to their own employees can provide computer conferencing on their own internal network
- open learning providers with their own computer systems can install conferencing software and then, using modems, make that system available to learners over the telephone network
- those organizations that cannot use either of the two approaches above can rent access to conferencing software on other systems.

From the management point of view, there seem to be two key issues:

1. The training of tutors: 'Computer conferencing requires a certain degree of familiarity with the system commands and architecture, but most teachers express a wish for more training in how to moderate conferences – promoting discussion, devising activities and encouraging interaction.' (Mason, 1994, p.43)

Table 3.5 *Management issues arising from telephone use*

Type of telephone communication	Examples of management issues
Learner to central organization	Learners need to be told: • which number(s) to use • for which purposes to contact the centre • whom to contact • the office hours • whether requests can be left on an answerphone outside these hours
Learner to tutor	Learners need to be told: • the tutor's telephone number(s) • for which purposes to contact their tutors • when they may contact their tutors, eg, are tutors to suggest convenient times?
Other learner use	Learners need to be told whether the course will involve them in other use of a phone, eg, • for e-mail or Internet group use • to access databases
Tutors to central organization	Tutors need to be told: • which number(s) to use • for which purposes to contact the centre • whom to contact • the office hours • whether requests can be left on an answerphone outside these hours
Tutors to individual learners	Tutors need to be told: • the telephone numbers of their learners (and when available) • for what purposes they are expected to phone learners • who will pay the costs of the call
Tutors to groups of learners (conference calls)	Tutors need to be told whether the organization wishes them to run conference calls with groups of learners and, if so: • who will set up the call • how much notice is needed • how long such calls may be • how the cost will be met

2. The support of students using the system: 'a more critical factor has been the tireless technical support of ACS [Academic Computing Service] and the ACS Helpdesk staff...' (Jennison, 1996, p.11)

Most computer conferencing systems are fairly sophisticated. The Open School has found that a simpler approach is needed for school-aged learners and has developed TeleWeb in response to this. TeleWeb, operated via The Open School's own bulletin board, offers e-mail, discussions and online chat in a simple, easy to use environment. Such an approach might be extended to those adults who find more complex communications systems daunting.

Using fax

All but the last telephone function (conference calls) can also be initiated by fax. In some cases, the response could also be by fax; in others, a subsequent telephone conversation would be needed. This two-stage communication may be thought cumbersome for quick queries, but is advantageous when the query involves something that needs careful study. For example, a learner wanting some feedback on an assignment outline would get better feedback by faxing the outline to his or her tutor than by trying to describe the outline over the telephone.

The specific advantage of fax, though, is its ability to distribute written information quickly over any distance. This might be used to distribute time-sensitive course material (see Example 16, on VIFAX), to set assignments, or to send in assignments. A number of other advantages of fax compared to the telephone and e-mail are listed in Davies and Gribble (1994, p.6).

Example 16 *The use of fax to deliver time-critical course material (Perrin, 1992)*

The VIFAX service of the University of Bordeaux teaches English as a foreign language to learners in French companies. The learners record BBC 1 pm news bulletins on Mondays and Wednesdays to watch later. On the day of each broadcast, the VIFAX service prepares four pages of exercises based on the broadcast and faxes these to each participating company to copy on to their learners for study on the following day. The answers to the exercises are faxed on the following day. On Mondays (the one day with no exercises to do) group discussions are held using conference telephone calls.

Where fax is being considered, a decision has to be made as to whether its use is obligatory, or is just an optional means of communication. Where obligatory, tutors will have to be provided with fax machines where they do not already have them and where access to a fax is not a condition of appointment.

If fax is to be a central part of the teaching and learning, tutors will need training in how to use it to good effect. Davies and Gribble (1994) illustrate the many pitfalls teaching by fax, but also demonstrate potential. While not a tutor training pack, Davies and Gribble's *Open School Good Practice Guide* could form the basis of, say, a half-day workshop to develop fax-teaching skills in tutors.

Chapter 4

Managing learner support systems

Learner support in open systems ranges from the very formal (eg, a tutorial) to the very informal (eg, an encouraging comment from a mentor at work). The overall aim of the learner support management system is to help learners use the organization's resources effectively. Ensuring that this happens involves three main management tasks:

- putting the support systems in place
- helping students to learn to use the systems
- monitoring the learners to ensure that they getting the support that they need.

The range of supporters can be wide, including:

- tutors (personal and/or subject)
- line managers
- mentors
- fellow learners.

Support can also be mediated via technology (eg, computer-based advice systems).

In this chapter I am primarily concerned with those supporters who are in some sense part of the system. This clearly includes tutors and line managers and can include mentors and fellow learners when they are a formal part of the provision. I shall not, though, consider those supporters who are totally outside the providing system, eg, friends and family, since the management aspects of such support are negligible.

Managing support from tutors (including tuition and feedback)

In most systems (and particularly systems with longer, accredited courses), the key supporter is the tutor. The tutor plays many roles although, arguably, some of those roles, such as assessment, are not part of the support function. To avoid having to decide just what is and what is not support, I shall consider all tutor functions here under the general heading 'support'.

Untutored, unsupported learners rarely complete courses, so most open systems stress the importance of their tutor support. Some students feel more supported in open systems than in conventional campus-based courses (Rickwood, 1994) which suggests that the effort put into support system design can be fully repaid.

Most systems seem to identify the tutor as serving five main functions:

- as a subject expert
- as a gateway to other resources
- to give feedback on progress
- to encourage/assist with personal problems
- to assess learners.

(The fact that this list is short should not be taken to imply that the tutorial role is simple. Lewis (1995) for example, identifies 20 skills needed by open learning tutors.)

For each of these roles, the management function is threefold:

- set up the role
- monitor and support the role
- evaluate the role.

Table 4.1 sets out these three stages for each of the five aspects of the role. In some senses, the separation of tutor as subject expert from tutor as provider of feedback is artificial since the feedback tends to be about the learner's performance in the subject. However, the skills *are* different. Subject experts do not necessarily make good tutors and many excellent tutors have just sufficient knowledge of their subject. (Given that the learning materials in open systems are the primary source of knowledge for the learner, tutor knowledge need not be the overriding concern in appointing tutors.)

Table 4.1 highlights two particular aspects of managing the tutoring function. First, new tutors need ready access to mentors, ie, to more experienced tutors who can offer advice and support. Just as being an open learner can be isolating, so too can the tutor role. Tutors may have no day-to-day contact with other open tutors and so have few opportunities to share their worries or to pick up tips. The mentor can help to fill this gap.

Table 4.1 *Managing the tutor support function*

Examples of set-up tasks	Examples of monitor/support tasks	Examples of evaluation tasks
Tutor as subject expert		
• Set standards for tutor qualifications and experience in the subject • Recruit tutors to those standards • Brief tutors on the course content • Train tutors in relevant teaching techniques, eg, telephone tutoring	• Arrange mentor support for new tutors from an expert in that subject • Monitor (via subject expert) the tutor's marking of assignments • Monitor learner feedback on their subject support, eg, on tutorials • Monitor student progress – lack of progress could indicate poor support	• Compare marks statistically against those of all other tutors • Review learner feedback • Review tutor feedback on the course and the organization
Tutor as gateway to other resources		
• Brief tutor on other resources available through the organization	• Provide subject expert support (ie, someone well versed in access to resources) to the tutor	• Review learner comments on the resource access they had • Review tutor feedback on their resource access role
Tutor as provider of feedback		
• Define feedback standards • Train tutors in how to give effective feedback in an open system	• Monitor learner comments on their support and feedback • Provide mentor support to the tutor	• Evaluate learner comments on the feedback they received
Tutor as helper with personal problems		
• Brief tutors on the types of problems learners have	• Provide mentor support to new tutors • Monitor student progress (eg, completed assignments) – lack of progress could indicate unresolved problems	• Review learner feedback • Review learner progress • Review tutor feedback on the problems they received and how they dealt with them

Table 4.1   *Managing the tutor support function*

Examples of set-up tasks	*Examples of monitor/support tasks*	*Examples of evaluation tasks*
Tutor as assessor		
• Brief tutors on the assessment system • Train tutors in any special assessment skills	• Provide an experienced assessor to support the new tutor	• Compare tutor's assessments against other indicators of learner potential (eg, prior qualifications) • Collect learner views of the assessment process and of specific assessments

Second, the table shows how difficult it is to monitor and evaluate tutor performance. Most open tutors work alone, from home or during occasional visits to other premises. Their 'output' is hardly visible. Most of what can be learnt about a tutor's performance will come from reviewing the comments on assignments and from feedback from learners. Given that these are the primary sources, special care has to be taken in obtaining this data and extracting as much information out of them as possible. Here, it is perhaps worth quoting one of my maxims of open learning: 'No news is not good news'. In other words, just because you have not heard from a student does not mean he or she is happy. On the whole, when open learners have problems, they blame themselves or drop out, rather than seek help.

Many of these tasks are new to tutors, so tutor development is an important aspect of setting up a support system. This is considered in Chapter 5.

Managing peer and group support

In some schemes, learners are encouraged to set up self-help groups. However, that is easier said than done, although there are things the organization can do to help such groups to start up and to work productively.

Setting up groups

A little organizational help can make all the difference between success and failure in establishing groups. First, learners need to be able to contact each other to discuss setting up a group. To do this, they need to know who else is taking their course, yet they will have no right of access to the personal details of the other learners on the course. (In a work-based scheme, circulating names without prior agreement is unlikely to be a problem.) Where this is a problem, the organization can help by:

- asking learners whether they are prepared to have their names, addresses, telephone and e-mail numbers passed on to other learners in the group – this is perhaps best done at enrolment or induction
- circulating the agreed list to the course members or, if the learners are widely dispersed, circulating local lists.

Helping the groups to function

Most organizations stop at this point, but there are other services that can be provided to such groups without trespassing on their self-managing aspect. For example:

- tutors can suggest aspects of the work that would particularly benefit from self-help group activity
- organizations can provide meeting locations for groups
- organizations can publish guides on how to set up and maintain groups
- organizations with computer fora or computer conferencing facilities can make those available to self-help groups. Indeed, such groups might only 'meet' online.

Managing support from mentors

Some organizations and professions (eg, nursing) use the word 'mentor' to refer to a workplace supporter who is allocated to the learner and who has some organizational responsibility for the learner. None of what follows applies to that type of mentor. Rather, in this book I use the word as defined in *The A–Z of Open Learning*:

'A person who accepts the role of facilitating an individual's learning. In its purest form the concept involves the mentor being chosen by the learner and carrying out activities as requested by the learner...' (Jeffries *et al.*, 1990)

Because mentors are chosen by learners and relate only to learners, management has no direct link with them and no direct managerial functions. However, as with self-help groups, there are three things which management can do to help mentors to work effectively.

First, learners can be advised on how to choose and use mentors. Most learners will not have had mentors previously and will therefore have no idea about what qualities to look for in a mentor or how to get the best out of a mentor. To fill this gap, an open system might:

- provide learners with an audio tape or booklet recording the experiences of previous learners and mentors
- allocate part of the induction time to a discussion on the role of the mentor – past students and mentors could lead this
- offer a system for linking new learners to past learners so that the new learners can get tips on choosing and using a mentor.

Second, the organization can provide briefing material for mentors. It cannot, of course, give this material to mentors since the organization will not know who the mentors are. Instead, the material will need to be given to the learners on enrolment or induction so that they can pass it on to their chosen mentor. Typically such briefing material will be printed and cover:

- the aims of the course
- an outline of the course content
- ideas for the mentor role
- an outline of how the rest of the support system works
- an outline of the assessment system.

Third, the organization can evaluate the mentor role in order to improve it for future course offerings. The lack of direct contact between organization and mentor makes such evaluation difficult to organize, but learners could pass questionnaires to their mentors, or requests to mentors to contact the organization in order to participate in, say, focus group discussions.

Managing support from materials

Typically open systems use a wide range of materials to support learners. These include the following.

Diagnostic tests – subject-related

Open systems often attract, or are designed for, learners following a non-traditional study route. One consequence of this is that their subject knowledge is likely to be more variable than for traditional learners and they can find it difficult to decide whether they meet the prerequisites of a course. One solution to this is to provide subject- or course-based diagnostic tests. These are usually designed for self-marking. Some are in checklist format as in Example 17. Others use self-scored questions together with a marking guide, as in the extract from the National Extension College French GCSE diagnostic test (see Example 18, page 55).

Example 17   *An example of an in-course diagnostic test for a course on presentation skills ('Presentation Skills Tutor Guide': University of Lincolnshire and Humberside)*

Read through the statements 1 to 4 below and tick the box next to the statement which best describes your experience of giving presentations and/or gaining presentation skills. Follow the step(s) indicated next to the box you tick.

1   I have never given a presentation and have never undertaken any study in presentation skills.

☐ Work through the student study guide.

2   I have given one/a few presentation(s) but have never undertaken any study in presentation skills and do not yet understand what makes a presentation effective.

☐ Work through the student study guide.

3   I have given many presentations and have learned how to do it well through trial and error and/or what I have picked up informally.

☐ Work through the checklist below to identify the key areas to focus on in the student study guide.

4   I have undergone a presentation skills course and have passed it (or completed it) and feel confident about my abilities.

☐ Attempt the recap activities (3, 9, 16, 21, 24, 25, 29 and 30) in the student study guide; work through the whole of those sections for which you have difficulty in undertaking the recap activities.

Checklist

This checklist is for those who have given many presentations and have learned how to do it well through trial and error and/or what they have picked up informally.

The following checklist indicates the topics contained in the student study guide. Against each topic tick either the 'Yes' or 'No' box to indicate whether or not you are familiar *and confident* with each aspect of presentation skills. For those topics that you tick 'No' against, the right-hand column indicates the section of the student study guide that you will find it useful to work through in order to prepare for the module assessment.

[The detailed checklist is not reproduced here.]

Example 18   *A self-scoring diagnostic test question (National Extension College)*

1 Vous avez _____?

    (a)   bière pression
    (b)   de bière pression
    (c)   de la bière pression
    (d)   don't know

[An example of one of 15 multiple-choice questions in the test, which also includes a conversation exercise.]

This test is self-marked and analysed against advice such as:

You have 16 to 23 marks

Whether you are learning for interest only or because you want to take the GCSE examination, you can confidently enrol on the GCSE French General course. If you are aiming for a higher grade in the exam, you could enrol on the General course and buy the pack for the Extended course without tuition to improve your chances. (For the highest grades you would need to complete the Extended course.)

[Extracts from the French GCSE diagnostic test published by the National Extension College for use by prospective distance learning students.]

Diagnostic tests – study skills related

Diagnostic tests can also be used to help learners identify whether they have the appropriate study skills for a particular course, or to help them explore their personal learning style.

The example from the University of Sunderland shows a typical approach to self-diagnosis of study skills capability (see Example 19).

Course guides

For some courses, and especially for longer courses, a course guide is provided. This usually serves the combined functions of conveying essential information needed at the start of the course (eg, how to contact your tutor) and providing other information that will be needed later (eg, how to enter for the qualification). Most guides are straight text; occasionally they are interactive, so initiating the

Example 19 *Self-diagnosis of study skills capability (University of Sunderland)*

Tick the box which most accurately reflects how you would rate yourself on each skill. Also decide which of these skills you want to improve.

	I am not too good at this	I have some skills in this	I am good at this	I really want to improve this
Organizing myself	☐	☐	☐	☐
Coping with stress	☐	☐	☐	☐
Locating resources	☐	☐	☐	☐
Reading effectively	☐	☐	☐	☐
Taking notes	☐	☐	☐	☐

[The first 5 of 24 questions in the diagnostic test for the *Effective Learning Programme* of the University of Sunderland.]

learners into the style of learning used on their course. Example 20 shows an extract from a course guide that includes activities on the guide itself.

Guides vary from the very short to the lengthy, covering from a few to most of the following topics:

- course aims
- course content
- course components
- course schedule
- scheduling your study
- how to start your course
- how to study by open learning
- how to use activities
- how to use self-assessment questions
- how prepare and submit an assignment
- how to use your tutor
- tutorials – when they are; their purpose; where they are
- using your mentor
- how to contact other learners
- how to get help – who to contact about what
- the assessment – how it works; when you do it; who marks it
- other resources – suggestion on what to use; how to get hold of them; when to use them.

Example 20   *An extract from a course guide (Study Guide for Chartered Institute of Marketing course: National Extension College)*

Activities and feedback

You will find that there are lots of activities in your unit. Most are followed by a feedback section.

These activities are there to help you learn. Most of us have experienced reading a chapter of a book and then wondering what it was all about. Reading is not a very good way of learning. Instead, learning usually works best when we try out the new ideas as we meet them. For example, suppose that you wished to learn how to write a marketing brief. You might just read about it as in column 1 of Table 1. Or, you could read about it and have a go at writing a brief. As you write, you will discover things that never occurred to you when you were reading. You will also develop the skill of brief writing whereas reading would only give you a knowledge of the subject. Finally, though, you might show your brief to a colleague and, through discussing it, learn even more.

The reading/telling way	The activity way	The activity plus feedback way
Reading about how to write an advertising brief.	Reading about how to write an advertising brief *and* practising writing one.	Reading about how to write an advertising brief *and* practising writing one *and* discussing it with a colleague.

Table 1   Three ways to learn about marketing briefs

Our example of brief writing emphasizes the benefits of active learning. The whole of your module is built on this principle.

Action point

Look at one of the activities in your unit. Note down: what the activity teaches; what the task is; and what the main point in the feedback is.

What the activity teaches

What the task is

What the feedback is

Key points

Scattered through the units – usually at two or three points – there are key points lists. These are summaries of important ideas in the units and you should find them very helpful for note taking and revision.

Action point

Look at one of the key points lists in your unit. Use the following list of ideas to decide how you might use the key points sections.

Read before studying the unit to get an idea of the contents. ☐

Check at the end of the unit to see how many I can remember. ☐

To make notes on. ☐

Turn into flash cards for use at revision time. ☐

Other ☐

Other ☐

Workplace guides

Many open systems are designed to use the workplace for a major part of the learning. Learners may need a separate guide on how best to learn from the workplace, covering such points as:

- which learning outcomes should be covered through workplace activity
- how to select a workplace project
- how to plan a workplace project
- how to gain the support of workplace colleagues for your learning
- workplace learning skills, eg, reflective learning
- how to keep a workplace diary or log
- how to keep a portfolio of workplace achievements.

The potential complexity (and hence the need for clear guidance) of integrating work and study is illustrated by Example 21. This shows a course map for The Open College Return to Nursing course, which integrates practical work with patients and theoretical study. Students negotiate their personal programme of study and carry out a project. Such openness, pushing the student to make many choices, requires extensive support and guidance.

Example 21 *The complexity that can follow from openness (Return to Nursing: User Guide/Project Booklet, p.14, The Open College, 1990)*

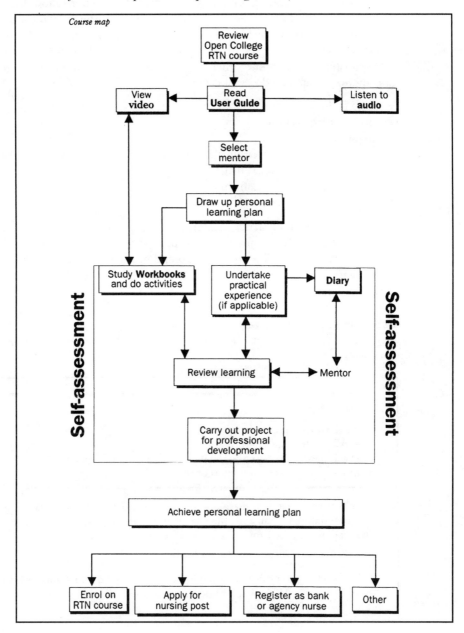

Examination preparation guides

Nowadays, many vocational courses are assessed using portfolios. When that is the case, learners do not need to concern themselves with revision techniques nor with examination techniques. Where examinations are used, both revision and examination techniques are important and need to be addressed either in the course material or in some other way. A guide to revision and examinations is one approach. Such guides may cover:

- why revision matters
- how to plan revision
- revision methods
- the structure of the examination (eg, number of questions, range of choice)
- how the examination is marked
- how to practise for examinations
- practice examination papers.

Some schemes offer a practice examination paper marking service.

Example 22 is an extract from a seven-page revision guide for the NLC (Off-Licence) examination. This comes at the end of a short knowledge-based course in preparation for a 30-minute paper. The revision advice therefore needs to be crisp and practical.

Example 22.   *Revision advice at the end of a short, knowledge-based course (The National Licensee's Certificate Off-Licence Self-Study Pack, pp.6–7, British Institute of Inn-Keeping)*

Revision tips

- try the questions and unit tests in the Workbook again
- make a note of questions you get wrong
- check these topics again in the Workbook notes and Handbook
- make up some exam questions of your own

After you have practised the questions, you should find that you have a good understanding of what is in the Handbook. The next step is to check your understanding by explaining the Handbook to someone else.

RULE 2: PRACTISE EXPLAINING
This second revision rule is a powerful way to understand something – explain it to somebody else. When you can do this, then you really understand it.

Revision tips

- find someone who is prepared to help you learn the Handbook
- give them the Handbook
- ask them to pick a topic
- explain the key points of the topic to them
- tell them that if they do not understand you, they must ask you to explain it again

PLANNING
YOUR REVISION   It is a good idea to make a revision timetable. This can help you make sure that you revise all the topics.

First, you need to decide how much time you need for revision. You might allow yourself one to two hours for each of the three parts of the paper. You might split that time up as follows:

Session	Time needed	Revision activity
Session 1		Exam part 1 – redo the unit questions
Session 2		Exam part 1 – explain it to someone
Session 3		Exam part 2 – redo the unit questions
Session 4		Exam part 2 – explain it to someone
Session 5		Exam part 3 – redo the unit questions
Session 6		Exam part 3 – explain it to someone

Chapter 5

Managing tutor support systems

Managing information for tutors

On any course, tutors need a wide range of information. Where a course is taught face-to-face on a campus, much of that information is obtained informally through day-to-day contact between tutors. Even when the tutors lack information, they don't have to go far to find someone who can provide it.

In open systems, tutors are much less likely to meet other tutors or to meet course administrators and managers. Indeed the tutors may work on a different site or, in distance learning systems, work several hundred miles away from the organization. In these circumstances, tutors have no informal systems through which they can gather information, so special care is needed to ensure that they get what they need when they need it.

Typically, a tutor's involvement with an open system goes through five phases, as set out in Table 5.1. The first two phases (recruitment and induction) will only occur once. Development, the third phase, may be concentrated in the tutor's first few months with an organization, but is likely to recur as the organization responds to changing learner needs. The final two phases (supporting learners and course review) will be repeated for each course offering.

Tutor information needs basically fall into six categories:

- *course information* – static (ie, what is known when the course starts) and dynamic (ie, any changes as the course is delivered)

Table 5.1 *Phases of tutor involvement and their corresponding information needs*

Stage	Examples of information needs
1 Recruitment	• course contents • tutor role • commitment required, eg, when tutors have to be available to learners • tutor development and support system
2 Induction (see Example 23, page 65)	• course materials – the chance to become familiar with them • qualification details and the tutor's role in the qualification system • mentor system – how it works • the learner system, eg, how learners get materials; what work they do; how they submit work • the tutor system, eg, how to contact learners; how to process learners' work
3 Tutor development	Tutor development is described in the next section of this chapter.
4 Supporting learners	• details of the learners assigned to the tutor, eg, demographic details; workplace details; mentor details; special needs • changes to course materials (eg, errata or updating material) • changes to assessment or qualification systems • feedback on own performance, eg, from a senior tutor or subject tutor • events of interest to tutors, eg, training events • learner progress details, eg, performance on computer-marked tests; performance on work-based parts of the course • changes in learner status, eg, changes of address; withdrawal from the course

Table 5.1 *Phases of tutor involvement and their corresponding information needs (continued)*

Stage	Examples of information needs
5 Course review	• a record of the final performance of each learner • a summative record of the tutor's performance, eg, range of marks awarded; average mark awarded • a summary of the learner feedback on (a) the course and (b) the tutor

- *system information* – who does what and how to get things done
- *learner information* – static (ie, learner details at the point of enrolment) and dynamic (ie changes to the learner during the course)
- *learner progress information*, eg, learner performance details
- *tutor performance information*, eg, feedback on the tutor's marking and commenting work
- *summative information*, eg, overall course results; results for the tutor's group; evaluative feedback from learners, line managers and so on.

More detail on these various types of information need are shown phase-by-phase in Table 5.1.

Managing the provision of information to tutors in open systems involves two main problems:

- tutors may be scattered over many sites (eg, on an in-company scheme) or wide areas (eg, a distance learning scheme)
- where courses are self-paced, there are no clear cohorts of learners so the provision of 'start of course' and 'end of course' information is problematic.

Possible formats for providing information include those shown in Table 5.2. The choice between these depends on balancing a number of factors such as:

- the balance between static and dynamic information in your system – print works well with static information; computer-based systems work well for dynamic information
- how quickly the information is needed – the post will generally supply information within two days; fax and computer systems make information immediately available

Example 23 *The contents of a tutor induction pack (New Tutor Induction Pack, The Open College)*

NEW TUTOR INDUCTION PACK CONTENTS

In plastic wallet taped to front of folder: Itinerary, Contact Sheet and New Tutor Reference Form.

Under the 1–10 Card Inserts goes the following:

1. Programmes & Quality Assurance Information
    OC Structure
    Pages 3–5 from Corporate Services Handbook
    Pages 18–23 from Corporate Services Handbook
    Complaints Procedure
    NVQ Internal Verifiers
    Telephone List
    Mobile Phone List

2. Training Materials Price List
    Corporate Prospectus
    Training Materials Brochure
    Training & Development Programmes Brochure
    Tutor Support for OC Management & Supervision Courses
    E&T Open College Distributor Network Leaflet
    Technical Brochure
    Professional Manager Leaflet
    Professional Manager Brochure
    CATT Brochure
    Focus (last 2)

3. OC Trainer Updates
    Tutor Focus (all)

4. Tutor Contract
    Standard Conditions
    Job Spec for OC Tutor
    Performance Spec for Course Tutor
    Performance Spec for Workshop Tutor
    Performance Spec for Advisor
    Performance Spec for Assessor
    Tutor Rates
    Tutor Fees & Expenses for Distance Learning Programmes
    Tutor Claim Form/Programme Update

5. System for Programme Set-up
    Professional Manager Set-up
    Tutor/Programme Briefing Agenda
    Tutor Brief Checklist
    Line Manager Briefing Agenda
    Induction Workshop Agendas
    Schedules
    Programme Review Agenda

6. TLS List
    Completed PMG Form
    3 × Blank PMG Forms

7. Tutor Report Form
    Assignment 8: Managing Resources
    Managing Resources (1618 words)
    Managing Resources: The Resource & Assignment Booklet
    Completed Tutor Report Form

8. Candidate Induction Evaluation
    Workshop Summary
    Management Assignment Guide
    Induction Pack

9. NVQ3 Grade Sheet
    NVQ4 Grade Sheet
    NVQ5 Grade Sheet
    Management Grade Sheet
    Supervisory Grade Sheet

10. Tutor Database
    Client Database

- how much labour your organization can afford – some methods (eg, loose-leaf sheets) are labour intensive
- how much storage space your organization has – ring-binders are bulky
- what computer systems your organization has – if you already have e-mail systems or some form of online access, using these for open learning may be easy to set up and of little marginal cost; putting in such a system from scratch may be too costly and require staff skills not available to you

- what computer systems your tutors have – except in in-company schemes (where tutors will generally have access to the organization's computer system) tutors are unlikely to all have access to the same computer systems
- whether your tutors have access to a fax.

Table 5.2   *Formats for providing information to tutors*

Format	Examples of advantages	Examples of drawbacks
Handbooks (bound or loose-leaf) (See Example 24, page 70, Example 25, page 71 and Example 26, page 72)	Good for: ● static system information ● static 'how to tutor' information	● if loose-leaf, bulky to store and distribute ● if used for course information, tutors may receive much information that they do not need ● poor for dynamic information since each small change involves a new page plus dispatching it to all tutors
Loose sheets	Good for: ● course information – tutors only receive what they need	● can be messy to store and distribute
Computer print-outs (See Example 27, page 74)	Good for: ● dynamic information, eg, learner progress record; overall course performance data ● particularly good if the computer is programmed to send only new information and changes ● despatches can be timetabled and/or tutor initiated	● messy if the system sends a mass of information only part of which is new ● costly if frequently posted ● can be out of date if sent in batches

Table 5.2   *Formats for providing information to tutors (continued)*

Format	Examples of advantages	Examples of drawbacks
Computer disk	• useful when the tutor needs to manipulate the information, eg, edit it for his/her learners • useful when the tutor needs to import the information into his/her own system • ideal for information that needs to be searched	• tedious for large quantities of information which has to be read (as opposed to being searched and read) • tutors must have access to a suitable computer
Tutor remote access to the organization's computer	• immediate tutor access • no chance of tutors receiving the incorrect information	• tutor has to initiate the information request • tutors must have access to a suitable computer with modem and communications software
e-mail	• good for short, immediate messages • for an in-company scheme with its own e-mail system, the system will already be familiar to the tutor • the tutor can access at home or work • it provides immediate tutor access to the information – no postal delays • it is likely to be read if the organization is careful to use it only for short, essential messages	• tedious for large quantities of information • tutors must have access to a suitable computer with modem and communications software

Table 5.2   *Formats for providing information to tutors (continued)*

Format	Examples of advantages	Examples of drawbacks
Computer notice board	<ul><li>easy to update</li><li>tutor can access at home or work</li><li>provides immediate tutor access to the information – no postal delays</li></ul>	<ul><li>boring to have to wade through a notice board, so tutors may not read it</li><li>tutors must have access to a suitable computer with modem and communications software</li></ul>
Fax	<ul><li>quick</li><li>can send existing documents</li></ul>	<ul><li>unless automated, labour-intensive to send the same fax to a range of tutors</li><li>tutors must have access to a fax machine</li></ul>

Example 24   *An example of system information for tutors ('NEC Tutor Pack', National Extension College)*

How NEC's system works

This is a brief summary – the forms and administrative procedures are explained in more detail in 'Surviving the paperwork'.

1 Enquiry
A prospective student makes an enquiry to NEC, by post or phone. NEC sends the *Guide to Courses* to enquirers and encourages them to seek pre-enrolment advice (by phone or in the form of specimen units, information sheets or diagnostic tests).

2 Enrolment
The student completes an enrolment form and sends to NEC. NEC enters the student's name, address and Course Code on their computer which allocates a Student Number. (If the student has enrolled via International Correspondance Schools the number is prefixed with a Y.)
An NEC Student Adviser checks the Enrolment Form for any problems. If there is any difficulty the enrolment is held and the student is contacted before the enrolment is processed. If the enrolment is straightforward it is finalised on the computer and a tutor is allocated automatically.

3 Despatch of course pack
The student is sent the following:

- Statement of their account/receipt
- Course materials
- Tutor details: name, address, and biography (unless details are suppressed e.g. if student in prison)
- *Student Book*
- *Exam Book* and Exam Entry Proposal Form (if appropriate)
- Essential Book Order Form (if appropriate)
- Course Card
- Assignment Forms
- Personal Details Form
- Student Enquiry Forms
- Two envelopes.

4 Tutor notification
NEC sends tutors regular notification of any student changes, e.g. newly allocated students or students who cancel or transfer. The tutor writes a 'Welcome letter' to all new students and writes a 'Follow up' letter to all students who fail to start within 4–6 weeks.

5 First assignment
The student sends first assignment to tutor with an Assignment Form, Course Card and envelope (unstamped), plus their Personal Details Form.

6 Marking
The tutor marks the assignment within 3–4 days, adds comments and grade on the Assignment Form, fills in the Course Card and returns the following to the student:
- the marked assignment
- the Course Card with grade entered
- the top (white) copy of the Assignment Form.

7 NEC records
The tutor sends NEC the second (yellow) copy of the Assignment Form in weekly batches together with the Batch Notification Form (a summary list of all assignment forms enclosed).
This information is used to record:
- that the student has done the work and the mark allocated by the tutor
- that the tutor has marked the work and will be paid at the end of the quarter.

8 Tutor records
The tutor keeps the bottom (pink) copy of the Assignment Form in their own record system.

9 Payment
NEC pays tutors at the end of each quarter: January–March, April–June, July–September, October–December. The tutor sends in a claim for any additional expenses (e.g. extra postage) two weeks before the end of each quarter so that these amounts can be included in the quarterly cheque.

10 Course completion
Towards the end of the course NEC sends the student a new *Guide to Courses*. On completion of the course NEC sends the student a letter of congratulations. A Certificate of Course Completion can be provided on request.

Example 25   *The contents of a guide for distance learning tutors ('NEC Tutor Book',
National Extension College)*

Contents

Example 26   *An example of tutor resource materials for use in workshops ('Tutor's Package' Appendix 1, pp.38–9, Inland Revenue Open Learning Branch)*

Training materials

These consist of

- a training manual
- a tutor's package

Training manual

The manual has been designed and written for trainees to use as a first point of information. We've tried to keep it as simple as possible, leaving out any points that can be explained more easily during a tutorial. But it does contain all the basic material and can be used later as a point of reference.

We estimate that trainees will need about 6 hours to complete the Administration and Tax Returns manuals.

The learning checks help trainees assess their own competence at the basic level. The answers include references back to the relevant text material. Trainees are encouraged to revisit the text if they get an answer wrong or are unsure about a point.

Tutor's package

This contains a range of material for you to choose from when planning tutorials.

The main items in the package are

- **Study objectives**

These are restated for each of the units in the manual.

- **Quick test questions**

All trainees should have assimilated the basic material before coming to tutorials but there will inevitably be some whose understanding is patchy. These quick test questions are designed to provide feedback about each trainee's general level of assimilation. We hope this feedback will help you to adapt the tutorial to the group's needs. The questions can be used verbally or in written form. The answers are available as handouts to trainees, if required.

- **Case studies**

The primary purpose of the training strategy is to make the training as job related as possible. To this end, the case studies deal with situations that we hope are close to those that the trainees will meet in their day-to-day work. Since Manual 1 – Administration gives mainly background to the Inspector's role, the case studies concentrate on the material contained in Manual 2 – Tax Returns. The case studies are designed to enable trainees to test their skills and knowledge of the duties of an Inspector to assess an individual's liability to tax.

- **PWs**

These are designed to give trainees experience in dealing with different areas of Law on assessing an individual's liability to tax.

Planning tutorials

It may help if we explain how we see the various elements fitting together. We would like to emphasise that we are not trying to establish a standard pattern for a tutorial. We expect there will be considerable variations in approach between tutors; what one accepts another may reject and, ultimately, it's a matter for individual judgement as to what is suitable for the group in question.

In broad terms, we expect a tutorial to

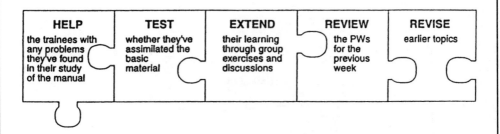

HELP	**TEST**	**EXTEND**	**REVIEW**	**REVISE**
the trainees with any problems they've found in their study of the manual	whether they've assimilated the basic material	their learning through group exercises and discussions	the PWs for the previous week	earlier topics

The order may be a natural progression for a day's tutorial, but the elements can be switched around as you choose.

Example 27   *An example of the use of computer print-out to keep tutors informed ('NEC Tutor Pack', National Extension College)*

```
T125

MRS D PRIME
KROKEN HOUSE
CRANES LANE
KINGSTON
CB3 7NJ                                  12/1/93

Please note the following additions and changes to your
student list.

Student    Course    Change                Telephone number

           E030      New Student
SS10830    MR A K TAYLOR
           3 NEWSOME PLACE
           VILLIERSTOWN
           WIRRAL             L56 8RE     0965 675 432

           ED32      Cancellation
SS 12255   MR J FERRY

           ED36      Re-activated
SS 12326   MRS G GEE
           17 EAST ROAD
           HESTON
           MIDDLESEX          TW5 0KN     073 764 981

           EO30      Deferment
SS16554    MISS M SMYTHE

           IC90      Transfer from another tutor
Y423786    MISS D SUGDEN
           FOREST HOUSE
           ELMS ROAD
           BASINGSTOKE
           HANTS              RG26 9TC    0986 653 231

           EO30      Postponed
SS453217   MR F FREETH
           279 BEACON ROAD
           WOODVILLE
           DERBYSHIRE         DE11 7KL    0954 632 786

           EO29      New student
SS 18443   JOHN BROWN
           HMP GARTREE
           GARTREE
           LEICS              LE3 8HG
```

Managing tutor development

The tutor role in an open system can be very wide-ranging and demanding as the tutor job description in Example 28 shows.

Most open learning providers use tutors who already know their subject well and who are competent face-to-face teachers; tutor development then concentrates on what is new in open learning. So, taking the RSA NVQ Tutor Award as an example of a face-to-face qualification, open systems can normally assume that tutors will be able to:

- identify individual learning needs (A22)
- prepare and develop resources to support learning (B33)
- agree learning programmes with learners (C22)
- facilitate learning through demonstration and instruction (C23)
- assess candidate performance (D32)
- assess candidate using differing sources of evidence (D33)
- evaluate and develop own practice (E31).

(RSA Examinations Board, 1995, p 7. Numbers in brackets show the NCVQ unit numbers for these competences.)

The new skills are likely to be some combination of the following, depending on the type of open scheme:

- building rapport with a learner at a distance
- helping learners to use open learning materials
- providing feedback to written work
- helping learners to respond to tutor feedback on their work
- maintaining contact with learners between assignments and/or tutorials
- using fax to teach and support learners
- using the telephone to teach and support individual learners
- using the telephone to run group tutorials
- running face-to-face tutorials for open learners
- supporting self-help groups.

(This list is based on the contents of Lewis, 1995.)

Developing these skills in open tutors is problematic because tutors tend to be part-time and are usually widely scattered. Often these tutors owe a primary allegiance to some other form of teaching and learning, perhaps seeing open methods as second best. Methods include on-the-job development, issuing handbooks, workshops and distance learning programmes. The advantages and disadvantages of these approaches are shown in Table 5.3 (p. 78).

Example 28   *A job description for an open learning tutor (The Open College)*

Job specification	**Open College Tutor**
Department:	Corporate services
Location:	Based at home
Responsible to:	Service Development Managers and
	Senior Training Administrator
Main liaison with:	Account managers
	Programme administrators
	Clients
	Award bodies
	Open College tutors

Description of role

Open College tutors will be responsible for designing, delivering and administering a professional and quality service of agreed training and development related activities on behalf of the Open College over a contracted number of days per year.

This will require close working relationships with clients and Open College personnel to achieve the clients aims and objectives for each contract to the standards as set by both the Open College and the various award bodies. Tutors will receive support and development from the Open College and will be expected to set high programme or consultancy standards that will be used as the norm throughout other Open College client based operations.

Main responsibilities

1   **To complete contracted work to the objectives and specifications as determined by both the client and the Open College**

Tutors will achieve this through:

• recognising and fully understanding client and Open College contractual requirements and determining actions for implementing and monitoring

• identifying the best practices and options available to ensure that training and development programmes are completed to obtain the required outcomes

• working with Open College personnel and the client on a regular basis, informing both parties of actions and progress to date including any changes for constant improvement

• representing both themselves and the Open College through professional and quality presentation of materials and training delivery when in direct contact with clients

- administering contracts by using and distributing documentation as required by the Open College, client and any associated award bodies

- liasing with other tutors, trainers or consultants, managing and being responsible for their contribution to a client contract

- identifying or accepting client contract problems and determining best options for resolving within normal job constraints

- completing contractual obligations in a variety of roles as well as making recommendations for improving those role specifications as covered in appendices a, b, c and d (attached)

- providing special duties and projects as discussed and agreed with the Open College prior to working with clients

2   Contributing to the continuous improvement of Open College programme delivery by designing and testing current or new methods or materials

Tutors will achieve this through:

- identifying, agreeing and testing new methods or materials and feeding back outcomes to the Service Development Manager

- designing and/or developing current or new workshop, learning, management or administration materials

- discussing and sharing best practice methods through to other Open College personnel for distribution to other tutors

3   Contribute to the identification and development of new or future training and development issues as well as developing oneself

Tutors will achieve this by:

- supporting and developing new and current tutors through attending tutors own or other Open College programmes

- attending and/or designing tutor development events

- updating their own awareness of new or future training issues or practices

- liasing with Service Development Managers and contributing to developmental plans and needs for Open College tutorial provision

Table 5.3 *Methods of training open tutors*

Method	Examples of advantages	Examples of disadvantages
On-the-job development	• cheap • new tutors can make an immediate start • tutors not put off by prior training period	• may result in poor tutoring in the initial stages • tutors may continue to use inappropriate methods
Tutor handbooks	• cheap • flexible – the handbooks can be given to tutors as they start and used at their leisure	• hard to tell whether the tutors have read or put into practice the handbook contents
Workshops	• ensure new tutors meet experienced tutors • provides tutors with feedback on their performance in a safe, supportive environment • can transmit organizational culture and build a team • can adapt the content to meet individual needs • ready-made materials available (see Lewis, 1995 in the further reading section)	• can only run when enough new tutors are ready • expensive
Distance learning courses	• flexible – tutors can start at any time • ready-made materials available (see SCOTTSU materials in the further reading section p. 156)	• not an ideal medium for a skill that has such a high interpersonal element

The first approach, on-the-job development, reflects that fact that in some schemes there is no formal training nor any detailed guidance on the teaching aspects of the tutor role (most schemes offer guidance on the administrative aspects). Perhaps the commonest approach is the use of tutor handbooks, covering the sort of skills discussed above (Example 29 is an extract from such a handbook). These can be purely descriptive or can take an interactive approach with activities and self-assessment material for the tutor.

Workshops (see Example 30) perhaps represent the most elaborate form of tutor development. In one or two days a wide range of skills can be covered *and practised* through simulations (eg, marking mock assignments) and role play (eg, practising giving advice over the telephone). The Lewis (1995) workshop pack contains activities of this type. One particular advantage of the workshop approach is the opportunity to introduce tutors to organizational culture and to create a team atmosphere instead of leaving tutors feeling isolated.

Distance learning courses are also used to train tutors. Where such courses are not supported by tutorials or workshops, there must be some doubt about their capacity to develop some of the skills in the list above. The effective use of telephone tutoring, though, might be a solution to this. Some of Lewis' (1995) exercises on the use of the telephone could be adapted for use in a distance learning course for tutors.

Some schemes (see Example 31) offer multi-staged development opportunities for their tutors.

Example 29 *Advice to tutors on how to mark and comment on assignments ('NEC Tutor Pack', National Extension College)*

Looking at how you work

We view this as an important area of tutor support, and give it high priority. We look at the work of all tutors to see how the relationship with students is built up and maintained, and how tutors are commenting on assignments and dealing with any questions that may arise.

Most of this monitoring is done within NEC's Learner Support Department. It is mainly done via the carbon copy of the assignment form (the copy which you send to NEC – see 'Surviving the paperwork' Sheets 3f and 3g) but we may also ask students to send *complete* assignments (the assignment form and the student's script with your comments) to NEC for monitoring.

A large part of a tutor's comment may be written on the student's work rather than on the assignment form – for example, to correct a mathematical solution or to improve a diagram. We try to see assignments from all tutors on a rolling basis.

Each tutor has an individual voice and so we do not expect all assignment comments to be written in the same style.

Some indicators of a positive student/tutor relationship:

- **Speed of reply**
  next day   –   the ideal, very good
  0–5 days   –   good
  6–9 days   –   just acceptable
  10+ days   –   unacceptable unless there is a valid reason, such as a holiday.

- **Tone of response**
  Does it convey enthusiasm for the subject?
  A good rapport with the student?
  Is it in the form of a letter, opening with Dear X and signed at the end?
  Does it encourage the student to respond?

- **Tone of response**
  Are the comments self-standing, ie will the student understand them without the need to seek further clarification?

- **Answers to student's queries**
  Is there evidence that the tutor is answering questions raised by the student?
  Are these questions about: the course? study plans? future courses?

- **A supportive stance**
  Does the tutor open with praise for good points before going on to criticise weak areas?
  Are positive/realistic suggestions for improvement made?
  Is there a balance between encouraging and critical comment?
  Is it clearly expressed?

- **Grading**
  Does the tutor justify the grade given?
  Is the explanation heavy on jargon or in language the student can understand easily?

- **Awareness of the student as an individual**
  Does the tutor's comment show a sense of where the student has reached in the course?
  Does it refer back to earlier assignments? or ahead to future options?

- **Legibility**
  The best tutoring in the world is wasted if the student cannot read it!

Whereas Table 5.3 considers a range of methods in isolation, in practice the best approach can be to use a mix of methods. Perhaps the commonest mix is to provide a handbook for reference and ongoing development, linking this to an initial workshop for an intensive introduction to the core of the job.

Managing the development of other supporters

Who are the supporters?

Rowntree (1992, p.78) mentions the following as possible supporters for open learners:

- adviser or counsellor
- tutor
- mentor
- line manager
- technicians or workshop demonstrators
- librarians
- learning centre receptionists
- other learners
- friends and colleagues.

Example 30   *Example of a tutor training workshop (The Open College)*

Open College Tutor Training

**Monday 22nd and Tuesday 23rd May 1995
The Open College, St Pauls, Didsbury**

Course Time Table for Providers only

Day One	**10.00**	**Welcome: Alec McPhedran**
		▫ Introductions
		▫ Aims and objectives
	11.00	**The Open College: Alec McPhedran**
		▫ Outline of the company
		▫ Structure and contacts
		▫ Brief product range explanation
	11.30	**Tailored Learning: Joe Pettigrew**
		▫ Flexible learning
		▫ The sales process
		▫ Building and starting a contract
	12.15	**Tutor Roles: John Bruce**
		▫ The role of the course and workshop tutor
		▫ The role of the adviser, assessor and verifier
		▫ Identifying key skills and activities
	1.00	**Lunch**
	2.00	**Reviewing the Open College Products: Richard Jacobi**
		▫ Activity: feeding back on materials
		▫ Basic product knowledge detail
	3.30	**Coffee**
	3.45	**The Modular Approach: John Bruce**
		▫ How the modules of delivery work
		▫ Theory into practice
	4.15	**Giving Feedback: John Bruce**
		▫ Assignment marking exercise review
		▫ Feedback of assignments/case studies/projects
	5.45	**Day One Review: Alec McPhedran**
		▫ Summary of key points
		▫ Evening exercise and agenda
		▫ Open forum
	6.00	**Workshop Design: John Bruce and Richard Jacobi**
		▫ Designing an Open College Workshop
		▫ Syndicate exercise
	6.30	**Close**

Day Two	8.30	**Workshop Design: John Bruce and Richard Jacobi** □ Preparation for presentation
	9.00	**Aims and Objectives: Nic Byrne** □ Outline of day two aims and objectives □ Questions to date
	9.15	**Workshop Design: John Bruce & Richard Jacobi** □ Syndicate work and presentations □ Feedback and discussion
	10.45	**Coffee**
	11.00	**Managing a Programme: Richard Jacobi** □ Tutor involvement □ Roles and responsibilities □ Support through Training Co-ordinators □ Product Development
	12.00	**Contracts, Costs and Administration: Christopher Brookes** □ Contractual obligations and details □ Tutor rates and charges □ Finance, warehouse and development
	12.15	**Tutor Development: Nic Byrne** □ Reviewing standards of the OC tutor □ Planning the process □ Accreditation and moderation
	12.30	**Lunch**
	1.30	**Open Learning: Richard Jacobi** □ Introducing open learning to learners, managing open learners and 'problems & answers' □ Syndicate presentations □ General feedback and discussion
	2.45	**Coffee**
	3.00	**The Next Stage: John Bruce** □ Post course actions and shadowing □ Syndicate exercise – final queries & issues □ OC Account Manager contact
	4.00	**Course Summary: Nic Byrne** □ Review of key points □ Summary of actions to be completed □ Open forum □ Course evaluation
	4.30	**Close**

Example 31 *A development programme for open learning tutors (The Open College)*

New Tutor Training and Development

Interviews
Following successful interview, tutors must submit two references from clients to whom they will have delivered training or development work. Once satisfactory references have been returned, the tutors will be invited to attend the two day tutor training course.

Pre course work
Potential tutors will be asked to prepare an activity from a pre-determined list for which they will deliver during the course. The purpose will be to allow the course tutors to assess the new tutors delivery or facilitating style. Activities could be preparing a ten minute talk on open learning or working with a group of people to review an open college specific issue.

The new tutors will also be sent an assignment, assignment marking scheme, tutor report form and assignment booklet for completion before attending the course.

Tutor Training Course
A two day residential covering suggested topics as per enclosed sheet. New tutors are assessed during the workshop by the two course tutors for their suitability in joining and complementing the open college product.

Shadowing
Following initial interviews and course completion, new tutors will shadow experienced tutors and must deliver one short session to a group under the supervision of the course or workshop tutor. This is fed back to the Open College.

Workshop Tutor
First responsibilities will be as a workshop tutor working with an experienced course tutor.

Course Tutor
Once the new tutor is familiar with the workings and standards of the Open College then they will be offered either course or workshop tutor roles. The same process would also be used for NVQ work.

Special Project or Consultancy Work
Experienced specialist tutors offered special project or consultancy work after proven skills in meeting Open College standards.

Apart from tutors (see above), very little has been written about the training needs of these various supporters.

Methods for developing support staff

To what extent, and for what skills is it desirable or practical to train such supporters? In answering this question I think it is useful to divide the supporters into two groups: those who have a formal responsibility to the organization and those who do not. On this basis, Rowntree's list might look like Table 5.4 for (a) a work-based scheme; (b) or a campus-based scheme; and (c) a distance learning scheme for home-based learners. However, which column a particular person should go in will vary from scheme to scheme. This analysis shows that mentors, friends and colleagues are invariably *not* part of the providing organization. Given that they are outside the organization, they are unlikely to see themselves as needing development; equally, the organization is unlikely to wish to devote resources to such people. At best, some kind of mentor's guide might be published and given to the learner to hand on to the friend or mentor.

On the other hand, tutors, advisers and counsellors always have some formal link with the organization, so training can be a condition of their employment. Admittedly, where their employment is very part-time (a common circumstance), it may be difficult to get them to accept more than a minimal amount of training. With this caveat, the methods of training for tutors (see above) are just as applicable for advisers and counsellors.

Line managers, technicians and librarians share one thing in common when their open learning training needs are considered: they are all likely to see themselves as having only a minor involvement with open learners. Each will already have a full-time job with its own priorities and pressures. Any training offered to them must be limited to essentials. Even with this restriction, though, quite a lot can be achieved, as is shown by Example 32 from the National Westminster Bank.

Many learning centres are staffed by non-teaching staff. They need to know the systems and be able to help learners to access particular courses. They may in some cases even help learners select courses. Example 33 shows the duties of centre supervisors at the National Westminster Bank and the training methods used. Interestingly, part of the training is delivered using the methods of the centre.

Table 5.4   *Supporters' links to the organization for various types of scheme*

Supporter	(a) Work-based: part of the organization?	(b) Campus-based: part of the organization?	(c) Home-based: part of the organization?
Adviser or counsellor	Yes	Yes	Yes (but likely to be part-time)
Tutor	Yes (but may be part-time)	Yes	Yes (but likely to be part-time)
Mentor	No	No	No
Line manager	Yes	No, but unlikely that the learner has a line manager	No, but unlikely that the learner has a line manager
Technicians or workshop demonstrators	Yes	Yes	No
Librarians	Usually	Yes	No
Learning centre supervisors and receptionists	Yes	Yes	Unlikely to be a learning centre
Other learners	Yes	Yes	No
Friends and colleagues	No	No	No

Managing people

Managing people in open systems is generally the same as managing people in any organization. Thus, an open system would need to have well-documented systems for functions such as:

- job and person specifications
- advertising for and recruiting staff
- terms and conditions of employment
- identifying staff development needs
- meeting staff development needs (see Table 5.5 for a review of the methods available)

Example 32 *Developing advisers (The National Westminster Bank)*

Learning and development advisers in retail banking

This is a recently (1996) developed role at the National Westminster Bank. The advisers act as coaches to line managers. A modular development programme has been developed using 1–3 day workshops. Modules already delivered are:

- Background to self managed learning culture
- Consultancy skills
- Awareness of Investors in People requirements. How to be an internal assessor
- Competency awareness and application in the workplace.

Modules currently (1996) being planned are:

- Making effective use of open learning resource centres
- How to use relevant computer and other support systems, eg the Role and Development Information System.

Example 33 *Training centre supervisors (The National Westminster Bank)*

Training and supporting flexible learning supervisors

The National Westminster Bank's flexible learning programme is delivered using 300 computers around the country. Each centre needs a supervisor to look after the centre and the learners who use it. The duties of a supervisor are:

- maintaining booking records
- looking after visiting students
- updating courses and workbooks ['updating' refers to putting files on the computer and keeping physical stocks of workbooks; the role does not include writing materials]
- extracting student data [for forwarding to a central office]
- providing the best possible study conditions.

Training for this role is provided through:

- a demonstration of the system from an experienced supervisor
- studying the computer-based course *The Supervisor's Guide to Flexible Learning*
- studying the computer-based courses *Quick Start Windows and Mouse Tutorial, Keyboard Tutorial* and *An Introduction to Flexible Learning*
- a supervisor's handbook.

- appraising staff
- planning and implementing career development.

Much of this can be achieved through the Investors in People programme which provides a clear structure for good practice in staff development. The methods needed for managing people are the same in open systems as in any type of employment and so will not be discussed in more detail here.

Table 5.5 *Methods of staff development (Freeman, 1996, p.45)*

Development method	Strengths	Weaknesses	Consider for
Full- or part-time taught courses requiring attendance at an institution	• Systematic • Brings in experience from other institutions • Usually certificated	• Needs time-off • Expensive • May not relate well to organization's needs	• Meeting individual rather than organizational needs • Meeting long-term rather than short-term needs
Open and distance learning courses based on learning materials supplied to the learner and supported by a tutor with whom the learner has occasional contact	• Systematic • Brings in experience from other institutions • Usually certificated • Fits around work	• Demanding for the individual • May not relate well to organization's needs	• Meeting individual rather than organizational needs • Meeting long-term rather than short-term needs
Secondments or attachments, eg, to another organization	• Can arrange at short-notice • Ensures practical, relevant development	• Content hard to control • No certification	• When time is of the essence
On-the-job programmes, eg, a learning assignment or a project,	• Very high relevance to organization's work	• Demanding on whoever supervises the programme	• When a keen supervisor (appropriately trained) is available

Table 5.5 *Methods of staff development (Freeman, 1996, p.45) (continued)*

Development method	Strengths	Weaknesses	Consider for
supported either by a member of the team or by someone outside the team such as a tutor at a local university. (When supported by a manager, this is often called 'coaching')	• Helps maintain motivation	• May interfere with the work • May be limited by the organization's collective experience, but could seek help from outside the organization	• When relevance to the organiza-tion's work is paramount • When you are sure the organiza-tion has enough experience to meet the need
Individual research programmes, usually supervised by a local university	• Individual gets what she or he wants • Accesses other experience • Certificated	• May have little relevance to the organization's needs	• To meet individual's long-term needs
One or more brief instructional sessions where an experienced person passes on knowledge and skills to an inexperienced person	• Quick • Highly relevant to the organization's work	• May lack theoretical background • May lead to doing without questioning or understanding	• To meet small, immediate needs
Working alongside another person in the organization – usually called 'sitting by Nellie'	• Easy to arrange • Can help team-building	• May be experience without learning • Limited by the teaching skills of the person used • Can perpetuate bad practice	• When it is your only option, or • If well supported by some more systematic study and reflection

Chapter 6

Managing assessment systems

In many open systems the providing organization is involved in assessing learners and so has to manage this process. This chapter looks at the issues which arise from this.

(Some open systems have no formal assessment for learners; others prepare learners for examinations of national awarding bodies, eg, preparing learners for GCSE examinations. On the whole, the management of such assessments falls on the examining body rather than the providing organization and so is outside the scope of this book.)

There are four aspects of an assessment which might affect how it might be managed: these are set out in Table 6.1. Column 1 lists four major descriptors of assessment methods. In devising any assessment, a design choice has to be taken on each of these factors. Column 2 lists some of the possible design choices for each factor. Each of these choices has management implications. These implications are discussed in more detail in this chapter.

The management of assessed tutor-marked assignments

Where assessed tutor-marked assignments are used, the types of question tend to be those where advance knowledge of the question will not lead to security problems. For example, questions can be set which require learners to show how they have applied the subject matter of the course to their work.

Table 6.1   *Assessment characteristics which affect the management of assessment*

Aspect	Some possible design choices
The format of the assessment	For example: • assessed tutor-marked assignments • computer-administered tests • closed-book examinations • open-book examinations • portfolio-based assessments (as in S/NVQs) • negotiated assessments where learner and tutor agree the format that the assessment will take
When the test may be taken	For example: • on demand • at fixed times determined by the organization
How frequently the assessment may be taken	For example: • once only • a limited number of times, eg, once plus one resit • as many times as the learner wishes (as with the driving test)
The size of chunk that has to be taken	For example: • learners have to do all the assessment on one occasion • learners can take each part when they are ready • resits need only be taken for the failed parts

The other management aspects that need to be considered and planned for are:

• the provision of clear assessment criteria to both learners and tutors. Learners need these when they receive the assignment question; tutors need the criteria at the same time so that they can deal with any learner queries. In practice, it is safer to send the question and criteria to tutors a little before they go to learners

- the provision of marking guidelines to tutors (if these are needed in addition to the criteria). In distance systems, tutors are unlikely to be able to meet for moderation meetings so the initial marking needs to be as consistent as it can possibly be made. Such guidelines may be:
  - general, covering all pieces of work on one course
  - assignment-specific
  - question-specific
- the provision of suitable feedback forms with sufficient copies (eg, one for the tutor, one for the learner and one for the central records). Standardized forms speed up the work for tutors, give learners a clear idea of what to expect, and help tutors to work to the system's standards
- for learners and tutors, the provision of a clear timetable for the assignment submission (unless the assessment is on demand)
- tutors need clear rules for dealing with requests for extensions and appeals over gradings
- tutors also need a help-line for assistance with problems
- tutors need to know what to do with the marks
- learners need to know when and how they will be notified of their marks.

The management of computer-based tests

Assessments taken using a computer offer the following advantages:

- they do not require any staff time at the point of delivery
- they can be taken by learners whenever they are ready
- the test can be varied by the computer so that no two learners take exactly the same test – this helps keeps the questions secure
- the computer can be programmed to monitor the total responses and to weed out questions that are ineffective
- marks can be logged automatically, being allocated to the learners' records and sent to their tutors
- learners can be given immediate feedback
- where the test is suitable, learners can take it as many times as they like.

Such systems are used to provide learners with one of three levels of marketing and feedback:

- a single mark for the whole of a test, eg, 8 out 10, with or without some general feedback
- a mark for the whole test, with or without some general feedback, plus the right answer for each question

- a mark for the whole test, plus the learner's performance on each question, plus some feedback on each question.

Such systems are of three basic types:

- *Online assessments*: tests where the learners interact directly with the computer (even if over a telephone line) and the computer marks the test online (see Example 34)
- *Online submission*: tests where the learners submit their work via a computer, but where the work is marked off-screen by tutors
- *Tests without computer contact*: tests where the learner has no immediate link with the computer, eg, learners enter their answers on machine-readable forms which are processed by a computer. Learners are then given their marks and feedback either by their tutor or using a print-out from the computer.

The postal systems are limited to multiple-choice questions and to providing feedback based on learners' choices of answer (Baker, 1983; Freeman 1983;

Example 34   *Using a computer to answer questions at a keyboard (University of Lincolnshire and Humberside)*

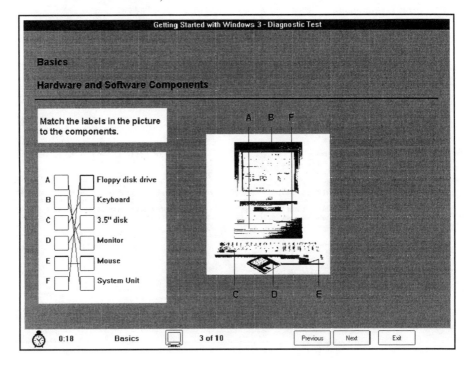

Mullett, 1983). Online systems offer the possibility of more sophisticated questions. For example, a 'question' could be a simulation (say a traffic management problem) and the 'answer' is a measure of how well the student balanced a number of competing variables.

Online assessments

Tests of this type seem largely to use multiple-choice questions. A typical screen presentation format is shown in Example 35. More complex questions can also be marked online and examples of how these can be constructed using HTML can be seen on the Internet at *http://medweb.bham.ac.uk/http/caa/newdb*. A typical question from the business and finance database at that site can be seen in Example 36. Here, the question format can accept a free response and the learner can request hints.

Some schemes have developed more complex online assessments. For example, the AQ system developed at the University of Lincolnshire and Humberside

Example 35   *An example of an online multiple-choice question (University of Birmingham)*

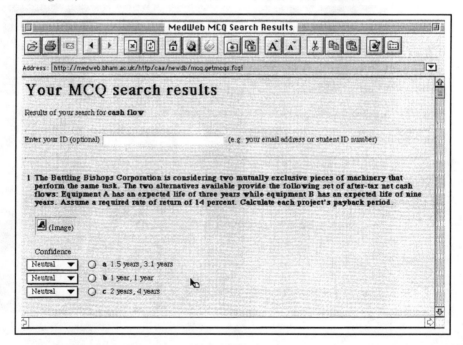

Example 36   *An example of a more complex online question format (University of Birmingham)*

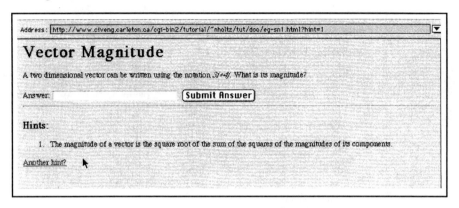

provides detailed feedback on tests of basic IT skills. Students can take these IT tests at any time, using one of the university's networked computers. Example 37 shows how such a test works for word-processing. Experience of developing and running this system has shown that the main management issues arise from the computer system. On trying to take a test, students may find that the Intranet server is not available, or that the server holding the AQ system is not available. Sometimes there are problems with the e-mail system, which is also involved in the assessment. For these (and other) reasons, students take the tests in locations where learning support staff are available to advise on technical problems. Difficulties have also arisen from students not reading the information sheets. Again, learning support staff can help here.

This University of Lincolnshire and Humberside experience is of online on-campus assessment and so illustrates the issues in a supported environment. If such a system were to be used at a distance, other issues might arise. As yet, there seems to be little experience of this type to draw on.

Getting the test ready for use

Once the test is written in a form which can be computer delivered, the following steps need to be taken:

- place the test on the computer system
- trial it with a few students – any problems in the test will cause immense worry to learners so you need to be sure that it runs as it is meant to
- inform learners of when and where the test can be taken; how often; and how they will receive their results

Example 37   *Online, on-demand assessment of word-processing (University of Lincolnshire and Humberside)*

Online assessment of word-processing skills

- Students are provided with an instruction sheet for taking the test. This sheet can be printed from the University's Intranet system.
- On starting the test, a title page appears. This automatically launches Word (the word-processing programme used for this test).
- The computer opens a Word document for the test.
- The student then types in his or her test answer (see Example 38 for an example of what might be typed in).
- The screen looks, to the student, just like Word with a few buttons disabled. In reality, it is Word with a set of macros (additional mini-programs) which enable Word to monitor what the students type, to mark their work and to give feedback.
- On completion of the test, the computer marks the test and provides students with feedback as in Example 39.

Example 38   *An example of a student's word-processing test entry (University of Lincolnshire and Humberside)*

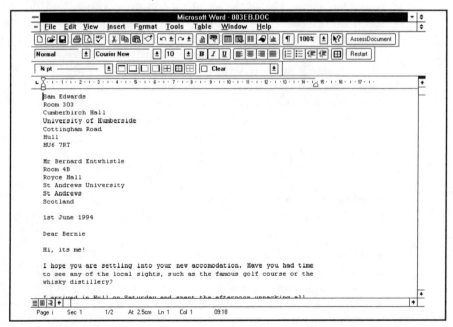

Example 39   *Feedback for the online assessment of word-processing (University of Lincolnshire and Humberside)*

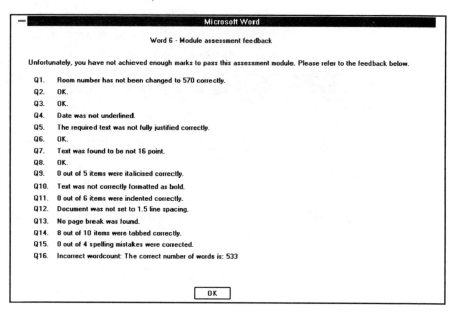

Microsoft Word

Word 6 - Module assessment feedback

Unfortunately, you have not achieved enough marks to pass this assessment module. Please refer to the feedback below.

Q1.   Room number has not been changed to 570 correctly.
Q2.   OK.
Q3.   OK.
Q4.   Date was not underlined.
Q5.   The required text was not fully justified correctly.
Q6.   OK.
Q7.   Text was found to be not 16 point.
Q8.   OK.
Q9.   0 out of 5 items were italicised correctly.
Q10. Text was not correctly formatted as bold.
Q11. 0 out of 6 items were indented correctly.
Q12. Document was not set to 1.5 line spacing.
Q13. No page break was found.
Q14. 8 out of 10 items were tabbed correctly.
Q15. 0 out of 4 spelling mistakes were corrected.
Q16. Incorrect wordcount: The correct number of words is: 533

OK

- provide a source of help for learner queries and problems. Typical problems include:
  - learners who cannot find the test on the system
  - learners who find they cannot access the test (eg, they may have an out-of-date personal ID or be using the wrong password)
  - unexpected responses from the test (eg, strange error messages)
  - system crashes while the learner is taking the test
- brief the people who will support the learners, advising them of any problems that should be reported to you.

Online submission

Online submission of assignments is becoming more common, especially among the virtual universities. In these systems, learners need to be competent in a range of IT skills. For example, to submit an assignment a learner might have to (a) prepare it using appropriate software (eg, a particular word-processing application); (b) call up an appropriate e-mail system; and (c) submit the assignment as an

Example 40 *The online submission of practice exercises and assignments (University of Monash)*

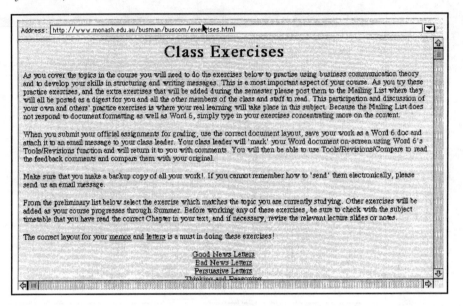

attachment to an e-mail message. An example of this approach to online assessment of practice exercises and assignments can be seen in Example 40.

Online submission raises new issues for the management of open systems; for example:

- Do learners have the right equipment both to prepare the assignments and to submit them?
- If learners are using attached files, can these be read by the centre, or are there hidden compatibility problems which will only appear with the first assignment?
- How can the instructions for submission be piloted to ensure that all learners will be able to follow them?
- Will learners be deflected from writing a good assignment by the complexities of the technology?
- Should a more traditional mode of submission be offered as an option?
- Should a help-line be provided for learners who have problems with submitting assignments?
- Are tutors confident and competent in handling online submissions?
- How can the centre verify that the submission is the learner's own work?

Tests without computer contact

These systems are usually ones where learners answer questions set on paper, record their answers using a form designed for optical mark reading, and send their form to the organization to be computer-marked.

The management issues in this case are:

- the test needs to be placed on the computer system well ahead of when the first responses are due to arrive
- once on the computer, the test needs to be checked to ensure that the computer correctly implements the marking scheme and that the forms run smoothly through the system
- the staff using the system need an opportunity to gain enough experience of it to cope with the common problems such as:
  - forms with missing data, eg, missing learner and course numbers
  - forms which are too crumpled to go through the reader
  - markings on the forms which do not correspond to what the system requires
  - learners marking more or fewer choices for a given question than the question permits
- the instructions for learners need piloting – one vague instruction can lead to a lot of extra work and many disgruntled learners
- if your tutors are expected to answer queries about the computer-marked tests, they need to be briefed well in advance of the issue of each test.

The management of examinations

Some open systems use closed assessment. For example, some universities offer resource-based courses which learners can study in their own time but which prepare learners for a traditional examination taken at a fixed time. Where this is the case, there are no special management aspects arising from the open aspects of the course.

In other systems, providing examinations is more complex. There are various reasons for this, including:

- the learners may be widely scattered
- self-paced learners may be ready to take the examinations at different times.

Scattered students

There are a number of issues to consider when providing examinations for scattered candidates. These are illustrated in Table 6.2, along with some of the factors that need to be considered. The key things to decide are:

- where to hold the examination
- who will do the local organizing
- who will invigilate the examination
- how candidates will be informed of the examination details.

Table 6.2   *Management issues in organizing examinations*

Issue	*Examples of factors to consider*
Location	<ul><li>the basic issue is to decide whether to use your own premises (eg, the local offices of a company) or to hire premises</li><li>any location needs be generally satisfactory for examinations, eg:<ul><li>– easy to get to</li><li>– parking available nearby</li><li>– has a reception person, not only to receive candidates but to take incoming last-minute phone calls</li><li>– includes a suitable pre-examination waiting area</li><li>– has appropriate toilet provision</li><li>– has a quiet, distraction-free room for the examination</li><li>– is suitable for disabled persons</li></ul></li></ul>
Local administrator	The local administrator must be someone of sufficient trust who is easy to contact in case of last minute problems. This person will be responsible for:<ul><li>receiving the examination papers in advance of the examination and holding them securely</li><li>issuing the papers to the invigilator</li><li>collecting the scripts and the examination papers (if they will be reused)</li><li>delivering the scripts to the markers or to the organization</li></ul>

Table 6.2   *Management issues in organizing examinations (continued)*

Issue	*Examples of factors to consider*
	The administrator will need: ● a task list ● a schedule ● security guidelines ● a list of candidates ● invigilator details
The invigilator	The invigilator may be the same person as the local administrator, but the roles are different. He or she must be a suitably responsible person. Often, officials of some other organization (eg, educational administrators) are recruited for this task. The invigilator may be responsible for: ● verifying the identity of the candidates – this needs special care in open systems ● issuing papers ● starting and finishing the examination on time ● collecting papers and passing them to the administrator ● enforcing the examination regulations The invigilator needs: ● details of when, where and how to get to the centre ● a task list ● security guidelines ● the examination regulations, eg, what materials and equipment candidates may bring into the examination
Information to candidates	Candidates will need advance information of: ● where and when the examination is ● how to get there and parking arrangements ● how they are to prove their identity ● what materials and equipment they *must* bring and what they *may* bring ● who (and how) to contact in the case of last-minute emergencies (eg, a car break-down on the way to the centre)

The table illustrates that there is a lot of detail, all of which needs careful attention, in running examinations in scattered centres. While systems matter, the absolutely critical components are the local people running the examinations. These will usually include an administrator and one or more invigilators.

The management of portfolio-based assessments

A portfolio is a learner's collection of pieces of his or her work. In some cases, the work is too bulky to physically place in the portfolio and so evidence of the work may be used instead (eg, a photograph of a wall that a learner built). In other cases the work may be transient and so an account of the work has to act as evidence (eg, a nurse's account of how she or he dealt with an anxious patient). Portfolios tend to be used for work-based schemes and schemes involving negotiated learning.

Portfolios are ideal for use in open systems since they are a mechanism for presenting evidence of learning to a person who was not present when the learning occurred. Almost by definition, that is the situation in an open system.

From a management perspective, portfolios are little problem since they push much of the management of the assessment on to the learner. This is consistent with both the philosophy of open learning and the practicality of running open schemes. However, a minimum of management activity is needed if portfolios are to work smoothly. These points are discussed below.

The management issues in the use of portfolios mostly centre on providing learners with the right information so that they compile their portfolios appropriately. Depending on the type of tutorial support available, learners may have to compile their portfolios almost unaided, or they may have ready access to a tutor or other supporter for advice. Learners, for example, will have to make decisions as to what type of evidence they need to collect and whether a particular item is or is not an appropriate piece of evidence. The less support they have, the more difficult it is for them to make these decisions.

Generally, portfolio assessment in open systems will work well provided that each of eight aspects in Table 6.3 is considered and responded to. The first two items (the portfolio's purpose and the assessment criteria) are the two key ones and they drive the responses to the other six aspects. Clarity of purpose is essential. If the organization is not clear what the portfolio is for, then the learners cannot be clear either. The result will be a random collection of 'evidence' to little purpose. Once the purpose is clear, then assessment criteria can be devised. These need to be written in a form that enables learners to be clear about what type of evidence to collect and to assess each piece of evidence for themselves. The assessors should use the same criteria to ensure that the assessment is open and fair. Where possible, national standards should be used for the assessment criteria, although learners may well need help in interpreting these.

Table 6.3   *Management issues in the use of portfolios*

Aspect	*Examples of points to consider*
1. The purpose of the portfolio	Learners need to be told why they are keeping a portfolio, including such things as: ● how it relates to the course outcomes ● how it will be assessed and what proportion of the marks are allocated to it
2. The assessment criteria	As with all assessment, the assessment criteria need to be made explicit to the learners
3. Its format	● If there is a prescribed format (eg, A4 ring-binder with sections on A, B, C…) this needs to be stated ● If learners are free to decide their own formats, this should be made clear
4. Its content	Learners need guidance on what to put into the portfolio, this guidance being tied into the assessment criteria (see above). Among other things, learners need to know: ● the number of pieces of evidence that they need eg, 'For outcome 1, you need between three and five examples' ● the range of pieces of evidence eg, 'For outcome 3, your evidence should come from at least one home setting and one hospital setting' ● the range of time over which evidence should be collected eg, 'Your portfolio should cover at least a three-month period' ● guidance on the types of evidence to include eg, 'You might include: lesson plans; your pupils' work; feedback forms…'

Table 6.3 *Management issues in the use of portfolios (continued)*

Aspect	Examples of points to consider
5. Its processing	Are learners just to present the portfolio, or are they to process the evidence in some way? For example, 'You should prepare a table with each of the assessment criteria in column 1; in column 2 you should state which items in your portfolio contribute to each criteria; and in column 3 you should give your own assessment (with reasons) as to how well you have met each criteria'
6. Its presentation	• how is the portfolio to be presented? • to whom will it be presented? • when?
7. Its assessment	The assessor will need guidance on: • the criteria (see above) • what record to keep of what he or she has seen • how to record the mark or result
8. Recording	The organization is not likely to wish to store portfolios, so consideration has to be given to: • what evidence of the portfolio will be stored (eg, a tutor's assessment of it) • for how long the learner must keep the portfolio (eg, for possible appeals against gradings)

The management of negotiated assessments

Most open systems use the term 'open' to refer to learner choice of when and where to study, but offer no choice of content (other than between set courses) and no choice of assessment. In a few cases, though, the term 'open' refers to learner choice of content and of assessment. In these cases, systems have to be designed to manage the negotiated assessment.

Negotiated assessment is managed at two levels: at the management level and at the tutor level. The management activities at these two levels are summarized in Table 6.4 which, for simplicity, refers to a single learner although negotiated group assessments are also possible.

Table 6.4   *The administration of negotiated assessment*

Level	Examples of negotiated assessment functions
Management-level functions	<ul><li>set the parameters which define the standards for the assessment, eg:<ul><li>– hours of study needed for a unit of credit</li><li>– performance criteria for varying levels of award</li></ul></li><li>define the boundaries of what can be negotiated</li><li>create recording systems for the negotiated agreement and for monitoring learner progress</li><li>create recording systems for units of credit</li></ul>
Tutor-level functions	<ul><li>explain the system to the learner</li><li>agree an assessment plan with the learner</li><li>record what has been agreed, ensuring that both tutor and learner have a copy (in some systems, the central administration may require a copy of the agreement)</li><li>record progress</li><li>record signed-off results and register them with the central administration</li></ul>

As the table shows, the main management function is to set the rules in order to ensure that what is negotiated has value and meaning within whatever credit system the organization uses. The key parameters of such a credit system are likely to be in existence whether or not negotiated assessment is permitted, eg, hours of study needed for a unit of credit; methods of defining the standard of a learner's performance. (Statements of competence are less likely to be used for negotiated assessment since they tend to be a feature of prescribed systems.)

The management system also has a record-keeping function, but careful thought is needed as to how much detail needs to be recorded centrally, other than the final assessment credit. Data might be recorded centrally for two reasons: because they are needed for decision making; and as a safeguard against poor record-keeping by the tutor and learner.

Learners who are able to negotiate their own assessments should also be able to look after their own records. There is, therefore, little need to keep any central record of negotiated assessments which are still in progress. The one exception might be a record of the expected submission date, since that might be needed to forecast course completions.

Providing information on assessment

In this section I consider only non-negotiated assessments and the information that learners and tutors need about them.

Table 6.5 summarizes the sorts of information that might be needed in a well-run assessment system. Nothing in the table is specific to open systems, but the method of providing the information will be specific to each system.

Table 6.5 *Tutor and learner information needs on assessment*

Type of information	Examples of information content
1. Information on the assessment process	• how many items have to be done • when the items can be started • by when the items have to be submitted • to whom the items have to be submitted • how they should be submitted, eg, word-processed • other documents required, eg, an assessment form
2. Information on the assessment tasks	For each assessment: • the purpose of the task • the task details • the format (including length) of the answer • the marking criteria • the answers (for tutors only)
3. Information on the results of a given assessment	For each assessment: • mark/grade awarded • explanation of how to interpret the marks/grades, eg, a chart on how to convert grades into degree classes • explanation of resits and appeals systems
4. Information on the overall assessment results	• print-out of results to date • list of items still due for submission • advice/warning of implications of results so far

Assessment in open systems differs from that in class-based systems in two important respects. First, the tutors in open systems are not usually responsible for the design of the assessment items. They therefore need information on the assessment just as much as the learners do. Second, the scattered nature of tutors and learners in open systems increases the risk of misunderstandings, so the information system needs to be very carefully designed.

The first part of the requirement (row 1 of Table 6.5) covers information on the overall process, including the number and type of assessments and the procedures for submitting them. Row 2 of the table considers some aspects of information on each specific assessment item – these information needs are the same as those for closed systems. Rows 3 and 4 deal with the learner's need to know how he or she is progressing. These data also enable learners to check that their results have been correctly recorded.

Methods of providing assessment information

Given the misunderstandings that can arise in an open system with scattered tutors and learners, there is a strong case for providing exactly the same information to tutors and learners (with the one exception that only tutors are provided with the answers, although these might be sent to students after the assessment). A simple and effective way of doing this is to produce an assessment booklet for students. The content of such a booklet is broadly column 2 of Table 6.5. This approach works on the principle that if you can provide assessment information that is detailed enough and clear enough for learners, then it will work for tutors as well. (The converse is not true. Writing an assessment guide for tutors is unlikely to yield a document that is comprehensible to learners.)

A particular aspect of this approach is worth noting: the section on marking criteria. For assessments to be fair, learners need detailed marking criteria. Criteria that are explicit enough for learners are bound to be explicit enough for tutors. Again, the converse is not necessarily true.

Rows 3 and 4 of Table 6.5 refer to providing information to students on their assessment progress, answering questions such as:

'How did I do on my last assessment?'
'How am I getting along?'
'What assessments do I still need to do, and when?'

(I have excluded from row 3 any reference to the detailed feedback on an assessment that learners need from their tutors since this is clearly not part of the management system, although ensuring the quality of the feedback is a management issue.)

Generally, such information is best provided from computer print-outs from the central administration since these are cheaper than giving the information in some other way, and students then see the officially recorded result and can challenge it if they think it is wrong. (Where computer print-outs cannot be used, some other method of confirming the definitive result to learners is needed.)

Where such information is given by computer, thought has to be given to:

- which assessment reports the computer will generate for tutors
- which assessment reports the computer will generate for learners
- how reports will be triggered, eg, on demand; to a timetable; or tied to events such as the submission of a particular assessment.

Chapter 7

Monitoring and evaluation

This chapter looks at those management tasks in open systems that affect the whole (or large parts) of the system, rather than one of the specific functions discussed so far. However, this is not a book about management in general, so this chapter will not look at generic management functions such as business planning, budgeting and staff development. Instead, the chapter concentrates on two areas where approaches specific to open systems are needed: monitoring and evaluation.

Hodgson (1993) describes monitoring in open and distance learning systems as 'the systems employed to ensure the quality of support offered to learners' (p.77) and defines evaluation as 'the process by which we arrive at a judgement as to the educational effectiveness of anything' (p.47).

These descriptions encapsulate the distinction that I wish to make here, namely that monitoring is designed to lead to action (where necessary) to benefit current learners. Evaluation, on the other hand, tends to lead to action which will benefit future learners. (Thorpe, 1993, tends to distinguish between formative evaluation (which roughly corresponds to what I will term 'monitoring') and summative evaluation (which roughly corresponds to my use of the term 'evaluation'). This leads to two general rules of thumb:

1. Monitoring should be limited to those functions where changes can be made in the short term. No other monitoring data are worth collecting.
2. Evaluation should be limited to those functions where it will be possible to make changes for some future offering of the course. No other evaluation

data are worth collecting. (Others, though, such as those doing academic research, might conduct a less instrumental form of evaluation where the issues investigated go beyond the demonstrable needs of the system.)

These rules emphasize that both monitoring and evaluation cost money and can only justify themselves if the benefits from the subsequent changes are worth more than the cost of the monitoring and evaluation.

Monitoring

Monitoring can be split between that handled by the centre and that done by individual tutors. I consider central monitoring first.

Central monitoring

Except in very small or very well-funded systems, central monitoring has to be based largely on analysis of computer data that have been collected for other purposes. Gathering additional data just for monitoring can be costly.

Typically, monitoring is done at three levels, as illustrated in Table 7.1. At the overall level, the course as a whole is monitored to detect problems that might affect all students. At the tutor level, monitoring can identify particular tutors who are having problems – for example, being behind with marking, or not providing students with sufficiently helpful comments. At the student level, each student needs to be monitored to detect problems at an early stage and to take remedial action.

Table 7.1   *The three levels of monitoring*

Level	Typical question being asked	Typical comparison being made
1. Course/ programme	'How is the course doing overall?'	• compared to other courses, or • compared to a set standard
2. Individual tutor	'How is tutor X getting along with his or her group of students?'	• compared to other tutors or • compared to a set standard
3. Individual learner	'How is learner Y getting along?'	• compared to other learners or • compared to a set standard

In terms of central monitoring, these three levels can be explored by the monitoring of factors such as those in Table 7.2. At course level, there is generally little data available to monitor other than records of learners' assignments. However, progress on assignments is likely to be a good proxy for how well the course is running and so can usefully alert managers to problems. As with much monitoring data, poor performance will not necessarily indicate what the problem is; more specific probing (eg, talking to tutors and learners) would be necessary to identify the cause of poor student performance. For example, late assignments or low marks might be caused by one of many factors such as poor course material, poor tutoring, irrelevant or difficult assignments, too much material in the course, and so on.

Monitoring tutors is perhaps the top priority given that tutor performance is known to have considerable impact on learner progress. The two key things here are that (a) the tutor needs to return assignments quickly and (b) the comments need to be well-chosen, encouraging and in sufficient quantity; Table 7.2 suggests how these factors might be centrally monitored.

Table 7.2   *Typical monitoring activities at the three levels*

Area of monitoring	Examples of factors to consider in monitoring
1. Monitoring the course/ programme	• percentage of students still on the course • number of assignments completed to date against target figure • average mark on each assignment compared to target • reports/comments from learners and tutors, eg, notification of errors in course material
2. Monitoring individual tutors	• turnaround time for marking and commenting on assignments • average mark compared to expected level or 'all tutors' figure • quality and quantity of comments on assignments
3. Monitoring individual learners	• number of assignments completed to date against timetabled target • whether the student has any marks below a set level (or the fail level if there is a formal pass/ fail)

In general, tutors will be monitoring individual students (see the next section on monitoring by tutors), but they may find it helpful to receive computer data which alert them to learners who are in difficulties. For example, tutors may not spot that certain learners are getting behind.

In general, monitoring means looking for performance that is below a set standard, so before monitoring can start, standards need to be agreed. For example, systems might set standards such as those in Table 7.3. (These figures are purely illustrative and should not be taken as recommended targets.) The final item, student views, shows that standards can be set even for relatively subjective qualities.

Table 7.3   *Some hypothetical performance standards*

Factor	Examples of standards/targets
Students leaving the course before completing	< 10%
Assignments completed	> 80% of continuing students for each assignment
Late assignments	< 10% submitted after due date
Assignment average mark	≥ 40% for each assignment
Assignment turnaround by tutors	≤ 5 days
Workshop attendance	≥ 75% of continuing students
Student views	≥ 80% rate the course 'excellent' or 'good'

Monitoring must lead to action

If monitoring reveals that there are problems with a course, its tutors or the learners, then action needs to be taken. Clearly such action will depend on the nature of the problem and the options available, but some typical actions are set out in Table 7.4.

Generally, if the problem lies in the curriculum or the course material, there is quite a bit that can be done. For example, if a unit of course material has proved incomprehensible to many learners, a tutor or the centre staff can quickly provide a few pages of additional material which can be circulated to all learners. If learners are finding that the course contains too much material, they can be told to omit certain sections.

Where monitoring reveals that a tutor is having problems, a more experienced tutor can provide support. In the worst cases, learners may have to be transferred

Table 7.4   *Examples of actions which might be taken following monitoring*

Area of monitoring	Examples of actions
1. Monitoring the course/ programme	• issue modified, replacement or additional course material • issued modified or replacement assignments • modify the submission dates • use scheduled workshops to follow-up identified problems
2. Monitoring individual tutors	• provide additional support and/or training to the tutor • allocate the students to another tutor
3. Monitoring individual learners	• discuss (eg, over the telephone) alternative study approaches with the learner • adjust the learner's schedule.

to other tutors. One way to minimize the chances of such a worst case ever occurring is to offer effective support to the new tutor. The Open College new tutor shadowing scheme (Example 41) shows one way in which this can be done.

From the management point of view, the key issue is to decide who will be responsible for taking action on problems. Such people need to be in place before the problems arise and need to be aware of their responsibilities. At NEC, the role is carried out by editorial staff; at the OU by course maintenance teams. Other models are possible; what is important is that someone is responsible for taking action.

There tend to be three broad types of action:

• course policy actions, eg, 'Shall we drop assignment B?'
• editorial actions, eg, preparing an erratum sheet
• tutor support actions, eg, helping a weak tutor.

Each of these may only require a few hours work over an offering of a course, but failure to make provision for such actions renders the monitoring pointless.

Monitoring by tutors

In the above discussion I have shown how central systems can be used to monitor learner progress. Such an approach is, however, crude and can only identify fairly major problems, and perhaps later rather than earlier. Tutors, being nearer to

Example 41 *A form for the monitoring of new tutors (The Open College)*

OPEN COLLEGE NEW TUTOR SHADOWING FEEDBACK

New Tutor:	Session taken:
Client and Workshop:	Date of Shadowing:
Comments by:	SDM: Alec McPhedran

Preparation of subject	
Objectives clearly explained	
Relevance of session to module	
Group interaction with tutor	
Use of resources and quality	
Outcome of the session as required	

Overview of session

learners, are in a better position to monitor learner progress and to take action when problems occur.

Monitoring by tutors can be formal or informal. In formal monitoring, the tutor uses data such as assignment submission dates (or non-submissions) and assignment marks to infer that the learner has problems. Generally, problems only surface by this route when they have begun to be serious. Informal monitoring takes advantage of the rapport between tutor and learner to catch the problems at an early stage, so giving the tutor more options for remedial or preventive action. This suggests that management's priority should be to help tutors develop the skills of rapport-building, rather than to train tutors in complex formal monitoring systems. Monitoring can also be shared between line managers and tutors, as in Example 42.

Example 42   *Monitoring work-based projects (National Westminster Bank)*

> Many of the development courses at the National Westminster Bank include a workplace project to be completed after the course has finished. This work is sometimes monitored over the telephone by tutors. At other times, the learner's line manager supervises the work as part of the post-course debriefing.

Evaluating the programme

Evaluations in open systems tend to fall into two categories (Thorpe, 1993, p.173):

- baseline evaluations – ie, ones where the same data are collected for each year, or for each offering of a course
- specific evaluations – ie, where there is a need to answer a particular question on a particular occasion.

In terms of managing an open system, the baseline evaluation will need to be planned into the system. (By definition, the specific evaluations cannot be part of the system plan.)

Baseline evaluation

Baseline evaluation can be designed to provide data to compare current performance against a particular standard, or to past performance. The three main approaches are:

- comparison with current activity
- comparison with past activity – although care is needed if the student population has changed
- comparison with an absolute standard.

Examples of how these comparisons might be made in practice are given in Table 7.5.

Table 7.5   *Types of comparison in baseline evaluations*

Type of comparison	Examples of comparisons
With another current activity	• comparing course A now to course B now • comparing course A now to all current courses • comparing tutor A now to all current tutors
With past performance	• comparing course A now to course A last year or course A over the last few years • comparing course A now to all courses in the past • measuring added value, ie, how much more learners know/can do as a result of taking the course (see Example 44, page 122). This may require pre- and post-course tests
With an absolute standard	• comparing course A pass rates against a target pass rate • comparing tutor A's turnaround time against a target maximum • measuring the standard that learners have achieved

Comparison with current activity is the easiest approach, but perhaps the one that yields the least meaningful data. Knowing that course A has a worse completion rate than course B is useful, but hard to interpret. Perhaps course B is unusually easy, or perhaps there really is a problem with course A. To some extent the data can be made more meaningful if one course or one tutor is compared to all current courses or all current tutors. If course A has a worse completion rate than *all* current courses, then that does suggest that course A has a genuine problem.

An improvement on this approach is to compare current activities with historic performance. For example, if historically a system has achieved pass rates of 73 per cent with a standard deviation of 2 per cent then a pass rate of less than 69 per cent or more than 77 per cent would indicate a significant deviation from the past standard. (Chapter 4 of Rowntree, 1991, provides a good introduction to statistical distributions.)

In some circumstances you may wish to set (or have imposed on you) specific performance targets, in which case comparisons will be made against these. For example, you may be required to achieve a course completion rate of 80 per cent in order to qualify for course funding.

Consideration also has to be given to which particular items of baseline evaluation data are to be collected. This will depend on the mission and aims of the organization and on the relative importance of different activities. For example, an open system that uses a high level of tutor input and not much learning material is likely to put more evaluation resource into evaluating tutors than materials. The main areas in which evaluation is likely to be considered are set out in Table 7.6. All of these items essentially come down to two key baseline evaluation questions:

- For our learners, can we get better results for the same or less resource?
- Are there other learners for whom we should also be making provision?

As Table 7.6 shows, these questions can be addressed by looking at how the overall system performs, what the market wants compared to what you offer, how each course performs, what people think of the materials, how the tutorial system performs and how each tutor performs.

I have distinguished in this analysis between course materials and courses. This is important in evaluation since, to a learner, a course is the interaction of organization, materials, tutor, other learners and so on. Good materials can become a poor course if the other components are inferior. Equally, good tuition can create an effective course despite poor learning materials. Having said that, there are circumstances where materials need to be evaluated as free-standing entities and these are discussed later.

Once the focus of the evaluation has been decided and once the main questions to be asked have been agreed, you can then decide what data need to be collected. Baseline data collection tends to use the routine systems of course teaching and administration so as to avoid costly additional systems. (Also, if data collection becomes too intrusive on learners and tutors, they will simply not provide what you want.) A range of typical data items used in baseline evaluation is shown in Table 7.7. Nothing in the table is specific to open systems, but everything in the table is relevant to them. Most of this data will be routinely available or can be collected with minimum demands on learners and tutors.

Table 7.6   *Typical baseline evaluation questions*

Evaluation focus	Typical questions
The total system This level of evaluation usually looks at the aims and purpose of the organization and often compares inputs with outputs	Why are we here? What are we doing? Should we continue to do it? What is it costing per unit of output?
The market The market might be a closed one (eg, the staff of an organization) or an open one (eg, the UK market for management diplomas)	Are we providing what the market wants? Are we reaching the market cost-effectively? Could we reach more of the market?
Each course	Is it working well? Can it be improved?
Each set of course materials	Do learners like them? Are they easy to learn from? Are they efficient to learn from or are they too long? Are they accurate and up-to-date?
The tutorial system	Do learners like it? Does it support learners effectively?
Each tutor	Does he or she succeed in helping learners to pass the course?

Table 7.7 *Possible data to collect for various baseline evaluations*

Area for baseline evaluation	Examples of issues and which data might be collected
The total system – compares inputs to outputs	Inputs: financial performance, eg: • profit • cost/profit per learner • return on capital Outputs: educational performance, eg: • number of course completions • percentage of courses completed • percentage of learners gaining jobs, promotions, moving on to other courses, etc
The market	External market share measures, eg: • percentage market share (in learners or in money) • enquiry numbers and conversion rates • marketing cost per enrolled learner Internal market share measures, eg: • learner hours per 1,000 members of the workforce Demographic information, eg: • population demographics versus learner demographics for factors such as: sex; age; race; educational standard; grade in the company
Each course	The following data might be collected and presented against figures for previous years and or other courses in the same year: • number of enrolments • cost per learner enrolled; cost per completion; cost per award • percentage of learners completing key stages of the course, eg, induction; each assessment; the final assessment • learner performance on each assessment • number of completions/awards

Table 7.7   *Possible data to collect for various baseline evaluations (continued)*

Area for baseline evaluation	*Examples of issues on which data might be collected*
	• percentage of completions/awards • learner and tutor views on the course (see Example 43, page 121 and Example 45, page 122) • reasons for learners discontinuing
Each set of course materials	• learner views on the materials (see Example 46, page 124) • tutor views on the materials • experts' views on the continuing relevance of the materials to the need or to some external standard, eg, a qualification
The tutorial system	The following data might be collected and presented against figures for previous years: • learner feedback on the tuition system (as opposed to on their individual tutors) (see Example 47, page 126) • numbers of assignments processed • average mark awarded • average turnaround time per assignment • number of tutorials run • average attendance per tutorial • tutorial cost per learner and/or per completed course or award
Each tutor	The following data might be collected in order to compare each tutor with either all tutors for the current year, or some other baseline standard for tutors: • learner feedback on that tutor • numbers of assignments processed • average mark awarded • average turnaround time per assignment • number of tutorials run • average attendance per tutorial

Example 43   *Part of a questionnaire used to collect baseline data (The Open College)*

Please tick appropriate box to indicate staff member's current level of ability in each of the areas he or she will be studying.

Learners Name: _____

Certificate Level Titles:

You as a Manager	Low ⊔⊔⊔⊔⊔⊔	High
Communication	Low ⊔⊔⊔⊔⊔⊔	High
Teamwork	Low ⊔⊔⊔⊔⊔⊔	High
Managing Work & Staff	Low ⊔⊔⊔⊔⊔⊔	High
Managing Information	Low ⊔⊔⊔⊔⊔⊔	High
Managing Projects	Low ⊔⊔⊔⊔⊔⊔	High
Developing & Recruiting Staff	Low ⊔⊔⊔⊔⊔⊔	High
Marketing	Low ⊔⊔⊔⊔⊔⊔	High
Managing Change	Low ⊔⊔⊔⊔⊔⊔	High
Managing for Quality	Low ⊔⊔⊔⊔⊔⊔	High
Managing Resources	Low ⊔⊔⊔⊔⊔⊔	High
Managing Finance	Low ⊔⊔⊔⊔⊔⊔	High

Signed: _____ Date: _____

Example 44   *An example of value-added information in secondary education. The figure shows how much better (or worse) one school's GCSE performance is compared to its expected performance, given its intake. (Source: Curriculum, Evaluation and Management Centre)*

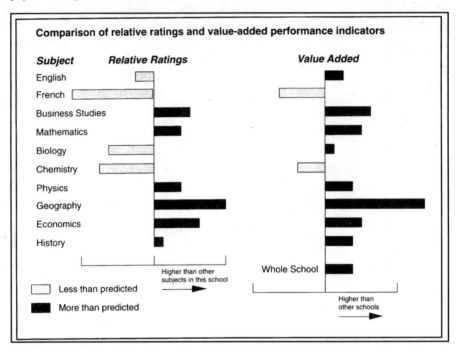

Example 45   *Part of a post-course evaluation form (Society of Cosmetic Scientists)*

Society of Cosmetic Scientists
Diploma in Cosmetic Science by Distance Learning

Course Evaluation Form

1   Please rate the standard of the following aspects of the course (circle your response):

	Low				High
Modules	1	2	3	4	5
Practical Activity Kits	1	2	3	4	5
Course text books	1	2	3	4	5
Audio tapes	1	2	3	4	5
Assignments and assessment	1	2	3	4	5

	Poor				Very good	
Tutorial support	1	2	3	4	5	
Administration	1	2	3	4	5	

2 Please rate the Modules in terms of content:

Module	Poor				Very good	Specific
Basic Chemistry	1	2	3	4	5	comments
Colloid and Surface Science	1	2	3	4	5	
Cell Physiology and Biochemistry	1	2	3	4	5	
Basic Microbiology	1	2	3	4	5	
Physiology	1	2	3	4	5	
Oils, Fats and Waxes	1	2	3	4	5	
Surfactants	1	2	3	4	5	
Gums, Thickeners and Resins	1	2	3	4	5	
Perfumery	1	2	3	4	5	
Oral Hygiene Products	1	2	3	4	5	
Aerosols	1	2	3	4	5	
Emulsions	1	2	3	4	5	
Hair and Hair Products 1	1	2	3	4	5	
Hair and Hair Products 2	1	2	3	4	5	
Skin and Skin Products	1	2	3	4	5	
Decorative Cosmetics	1	2	3	4	5	
Product Development	1	2	3	4	5	
Packaging – Design, Selection and Use	1	2	3	4	5	
Production	1	2	3	4	5	
Analytical Chemistry	1	2	3	4	5	
Product evaluation	1	2	3	4	5	
Statistics for Product Evaluation	1	2	3	4	5	
Legislation	1	2	3	4	5	
Product Safety	1	2	3	4	5	
Industrial Microbiology	1	2	3	4	5	
Quality Assurance	1	2	3	4	5	
Product Stability	1	2	3	4	5	
Consumer and Market Research	1	2	3	4	5	
Marketing	1	2	3	4	5	

3 Please give your impression of the layout of the Modules:

a *Size of the booklets* Too large/about right/too small

b *Size of the typescript* Too large/about right/too small

c *Number of figures, tables, photos* Too many/about right/too few

d *Usefulness of figures, tables, photos* Good/satisfactory/poor

e *Space for making notes/writing Activity answers* Too much/about right/too little

Example 46   *Part of a materials evaluation questionnaire for learners (Inland Revenue Open Learning Branch)*

Section One

1.1 Did the manual arrive on time?   Yes ☐   No ☐

1.2 Were the instructions how to use
the manual clear?   Very clear ▭▭▭▭▭ Unclear

Section Two

2.1 How much of the material was
new to you?   None of it ▭▭▭▭▭ All of it

2.2 How much of the material do
you consider will be of use to you in
your job?   All of it ▭▭▭▭▭ None of it

2.3 Do you think the material   Too much
contained the right amount of   Right
information?   amount ☐   ☐   ☐ Too little

2.4 Do you feel confident that you can
now meet all the objectives set out in   Not
the material?   Confident ▭▭▭▭▭ confident

2.5 If appropriate did you find the
examples used in the manual useful?   Very useful ▭▭▭▭▭ Not useful

Section Three

3.1 Did you find the structure of the
manual easy or difficult to follow?   Easy ▭▭▭▭▭ Difficult

3.2 Did you find the design of the manual helped or hindered your learning?

Helped ☐☐☐☐☐ Hindered

3.3 Did you find the tone of the material friendly or daunting?

Friendly ☐☐☐☐☐ Daunting

Questions 3.4–3.8 may not apply to all training packages. Only fill them in if appropriate.

3.4 How useful were the in-text activities in helping you to understand the material?

Very useful ☐☐☐☐☐ Not useful

3.5 Were our responses to the activities clear or unclear?

Clear ☐☐☐☐☐ Unclear

3.6 How useful were the learning checks in helping you to check your understanding of the material?

Very useful ☐☐☐☐☐ Not useful

3.7 Where there are recommended breaks, were the sections between breaks?

About right ☐ Too short ☐ Too long ☐

3.8 How many activities did you complete?

All ☐☐☐☐☐ None

3.9 If appropriate did you complete all the learning checks?

All ☐☐☐☐☐ None

3.10 If appropriate how useful was the study advice?

Very useful ☐☐☐☐☐ Not useful

3.11 Did you find the suggested pace of learning:

About right ☐ Too fast ☐ Too slow ☐

Example 47   *A workshop evaluation form (The Open College)*

Open College

Candidate Workshop Evaluation

Company: _____ Group No: _____

Workshop Title: _____

Location: _____ Date of Workshop: _____

Course title: _____

Course Tutor: _____ Workshop Tutor: _____

The Open College continually seek to improve the delivery of its products and services. As part of this process, we would welcome your comments on both today's workshop and the course in general. You are not obliged to put your name on this evaluation. Please use the back of this form for any additional comments that you would like to make.

Please rate the following with 1 for poor to 10 for excellent: 1–10

Workshop objectives met   ☐

Review of previous module/stage   ☐

Preview of next module/stage   ☐

Individual contact with Course Tutor/Adviser (if applicable)   ☐

Relevance of the workshop activities during the day   ☐

The next assignment/CDA/Unit briefing   ☐

Content and structure of the day   ☐

Open College tutors' training and presentation skills   ☐

Your understanding of what you have to do before the next workshop   ☐

Overall level of satisfaction of the day   ☐

Total   ☐

What activity did you find most useful and why?

_____

_____

_____

What activity was least useful and why?

_____

_____

_____

What do you need to do before the next workshop?

_____

_____

_____

Any additional comments you feel you would like to make? This can be about the course itself, the workshops, the workbooks, the support you are receiving, etc

_____

_____

_____

Name: _____ Work Tel. No: _____

Evaluating materials

When you wish to buy in materials, you will need to have some way of evaluating them before they become part of a course. This is the one occasion on which evaluating materials as free-standing items seems to be unavoidable. (You may, however, be able to get course performance data from the publisher of the materials.)

Example 48 shows an evaluation checklist which I have developed over the last ten years. It reflects the mistakes which I find new authors tend to make when writing materials and hence is a good indicator of problems that you might find with bought-in materials. Many other evaluation checklists have been published for materials, eg, Rowntree, 1992, p.145; Thorpe, 1993, pp.158–9; Department of Employment Training Agency, 1990, C1–9.

Example 48   *A materials evaluation checklist*

Aspect	*Present?/Yes/No?*
1. The course as a whole	
1.1 The course guide includes:	
Course map showing:	☐
• all course components and the relationship between them • when to use what • the assessment programme	☐ ☐ ☐
Course introduction describing:	☐
• the aims of course • the expected outcomes • the target audience • the prerequisites • the qualification details	☐ ☐ ☐ ☐ ☐
Pre–test	☐
How to use the course, including:	☐
• the estimated study time • study methods advice	☐ ☐
1.2 Objectives and qualification	
Do the objectives match the qualification?	☐

1.3 Course assessment (not self-assessment)

The course assessment material is clearly labelled ☐

For the assessment items, check that:

- when to do each item is clear ☐
- items only test what is in the course objectives ☐
- either that all the objectives are tested or, if not feasible, a sensible selection is tested ☐
- that each assessment item uses a method which is valid for the objective being tested ☐
- that the assessment uses the minimum learner time to achieve its purpose ☐

2.   Unit by unit check

2.1 Introductory items. Check that the following are present:

- a clear, lively, introduction ☐
- the prerequisites of unit ☐
- a list of the tools/equipment needed for unit ☐

2.2 Unit as a whole

Objectives. Check that:

- objectives are in behavioural terms ☐
- activities are provided for each objective ☐
- nothing is taught which is not needed for the objectives ☐
- every objective is tested with self-assessment questions ☐

2.3 Unit sections

- the unit is sub-divided into sections no longer than one study session ☐
- sections have suggested study times ☐

2.4 Activities

- are interesting/worth doing ☐
- seriously promote learning ☐
- are varied in style/format ☐
- do not ask the learner to guess what is about to be taught ☐
- feedback is given on likely answers ☐

2.5 Self-assessment

- each objective has at least one self-assessment question (SAQ) ☐
- SAQs do not test too much in one question ☐
- full answers are given ☐

2.6 Diagrams/illustrations. Check that:

- diagrams are ones which aid learning ☐
- some activities are set on diagrams ☐
- diagrams are used to reduce text ☐
- are non–sexist/non–racist ☐

2.7 Language. Check that it:

- is simple ☐
- is fluent ☐
- is clear ☐
- is grammatically accurate ☐
- is direct ('you', etc) ☐
- avoids the passive tense, except when clearer ☐
- avoids negatives ☐
- avoids clichés ☐
- is non–sexist, non–racist ☐

2.8 Miscellaneous

- unit summary present ☐
- flagging. Check that different study processes (eg, reading, video) are clearly marked ☐

3. Tutors' notes. Check that these include:

- the background to the course ☐
- the qualification details ☐
- tutor's role in the qualification ☐
- the assignments and marking guidelines ☐

Evaluating staff development

The choice of method for evaluating staff development is a difficult and technical issue which is beyond the scope of this book. However, the essential requirements of the evaluation process are:

- evaluation must include measuring the outcomes against the original learning objectives or the original learning need. Essentially, what you are asking here is 'Can... now meet the requirements of the job or task for which the development was provided?'

- wherever possible, agree with the learner (who, in this context, is a supporter or other member of staff) how the evaluation will be done
- wherever possible, ask the learner to produce evidence of what she or he has learnt – this both involves the learner in the evaluation process and is a powerful piece of reflective learning in its own right
- make sure that your evaluation process can detect unplanned outcomes from the development – both desirable and undesirable ones
- make sure that the evaluation is recorded in writing and signed by both parties
- consider whether any parts of the evaluation should involve other members of the team
- consider the implications of the acquisition of skills and knowledge. For example, the member of staff might feel empowered by the development. Are the team's systems and methods able to respond and adjust to this?

Quality assurance systems

Given that few open systems have formal quality assurance systems, perhaps the first management issue is, 'Should we have a system at all?'

Quality management systems

The choice is between two principal approaches. The first is to use a quality management system. Such systems identify the main processes in an organization, set out how these should be done (using such devices as flowcharts and defined standards) and then establish monitoring systems (called auditing) to check on the organization's adherence to the defined way of doing things. A typical quality assurance system of this type follows the flow of activity shown in Figure 7.1. Implementing and running such a system involves management in:

- establishing clear user requirements (eg, what the learners expect of the provider; what employers expect)
- identifying the key processes in the organization (eg, advising enquirers, making materials, tutoring learners) and then codifying the best way to do these things. This results in documents called procedures, backed up where necessary by more detailed and specific work instructions
- establishing an audit system for investigating how well the organization adheres to the procedures

- establishing a corrective action procedure for putting right, and learning from, failures to adhere to the procedures
- establishing a management review system to evaluate the system and change and develop it as needed.

Although quite a number of organizations have considered setting up such systems, they do not seem to have flourished in open and distance organizations. It seems that this approach, originally devised for manufacturing, is difficult to apply to education. Regrettably, there are no certain processes which, if carefully followed, will guarantee quality. The indefinite and intangible nature of teaching and learning eludes definition through procedures.

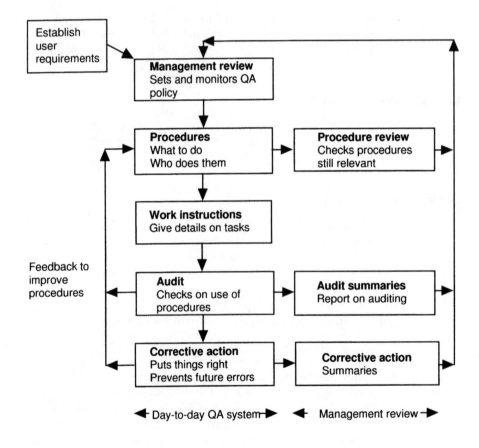

Figure 7.1 *An outline of a quality assurance system (Freeman, 1993, p.28)*

One area where this approach has been more successful is in the materials production aspects of open distance learning. For example, the Inland Revenue materials production system has been awarded the BS 5750 standard. An extract from their quality manual can be seen in Example 49.

Example 49   *An example of a quality assurance system for producing learning materials (Inland Revenue Training Office)*

Our Quality Policy

Purpose

The purpose of Training Office Production Team (Leeds) is to design, produce and procure quality training solutions for our customers.

Quality Commitment

Training Office Production Team (Leeds) is committed to providing quality solutions for our customers. We have therefore implemented a quality assurance programme as the means to achieving our purpose.

Quality Assurance Management

The QA system is the responsibility of the QA Management Review Group, consisting of the Quality Manager, the Customer Service Manager and led by the Head of Training Office Production Team Leeds. This group is responsible for all QA policy decisions and for monitoring the effectiveness of the QA system.

Day-to-day management of the QA system is the responsibility of the Quality Manager (see roles and responsibilities document). The QM oversees the introduction of new procedures, manages the audit programme, monitors the running of the QA system and reports to the Management Review Group.

Team Members' Responsibilities

Individual team members are responsible for implementing the QA system within their own work areas as laid out in the quality procedures. In particular, they should:

- ensure that they have up-to-date QA documentation (as defined below)
- familiarise themselves with the documentation
- carry out work in accordance with the QA procedures and work instructions
- maintain quality records as required.

The overall aim of the QA system is to ensure that our products meet customers' requirements.

Management Review

The Management Review Group shall review the QA system quarterly and in particular shall monitor adherence to the audit programme, the level of non-compliance and the promptness of corrective action. Where the QA programme is found to be ineffective or failing to meet customers' needs, the Management Review Group shall initiate changes to the system.

Our Quality Assurance System

To help us achieve the aims of our Quality Policy, we have implemented a quality assurance system based on the principles set out in BS EN ISO 9000. Our quality assurance system is designed so that we clearly identify our customers needs, we produce or procure the most efficient solutions to those needs, and we implement those solutions in the most efficient way.

We do this by following key quality procedures, which have been identified as being crucial to our commitment to meeting customers needs. These procedures form the essential building blocks of our quality system. Each procedure is supported by detailed documentation and specifications and the system is subject to rigorous internal audit and review, to ensure that customers needs are met.

The working of the quality assurance system is regularly reviewed by the management review group of: Head of Team, Customer Service Manager and Quality Manager.

An outline of our system is shown below.

PR/1	Setting up a project	
PR/1a	Pre-production planning	
PR/2	Production	
PR/3	Physical production	Design and
PR/4	Evaluation	Production
PR/11	Revision and amendment planning	
PR/12	Minor amendments	
PR/12a	Major amendments	
PR/5	Training and development	Administration
PR/6	Freelance suppliers	
PR/7	Management review	
PR/9	Document control	Quality
PR/10	Audit	Management
PR/13	Computer filing and archive	
PR/14	Handling complaints	

Total quality systems

The second approach, total quality management (TQM), is hard to distinguish from good management (if it can be distinguished at all). TQM involves all the staff of an organization in thinking about, and taking responsibility for, the quality of what they do and of what the organization does. The aim is 'continuous quality improvement'. Thus, the emphasis is not on codifying good practice but on continuously reviewing practice in order to ask 'Can we do better?'

Typically, TQM systems make use of a range of techniques, including:

- *Brainstorming*, particularly for producing creative ideas for improving the quality of a particular process, eg, how can we produce course materials more quickly to meet urgent needs from our corporate customers?
- *Affinity networks*. These analyse the output of brainstorming sessions in order to identify links between different factors, eg, brainstorming might identify all the factors which affect the quality of tutor feedback on assignments. Affinity networks can be used to analyse which factors are related to which others.
- *Fishbone diagrams*. These are a diagrammatic way of showing all the factors that impact on a problem or process. Groups can use these diagrams to help identify cause and effect, especially in problem solving.
- *Benchmarking*. In TQM, benchmarking refers to finding out the standard of your competitors and then using that as a standard that you aim to better.

Often, these methods are applied through quality circles, ie, groups of employees who meet in work time to discuss and solve quality problems.

Perhaps the most striking thing about TQM is the eclectic nature of its implementation. You can take the bits that seem to answer your current needs, try them out, and then perhaps do something different. TQM is, after all, more a philosophy that a system.

The management implications of TQM in open distance systems include:

- the need to be clear about what the quality goals of the organization are, and to communicate these to all the staff. This can be particularly difficult when many of the staff may be remote, part-time tutors
- the need to show a total commitment to quality and to support staff in developing their commitment. For example, if staff are to take a TQM approach then they need training in TQM methods, support in finding the time and resources to pursue these (for example, time for quality circles) and the management style needs to be highly participative.

Chapter 8

Managing investment

The one aspect of finance that is likely to be different in open systems is the need to manage investment. Open systems, especially those which produce materials, tend to have higher fixed costs and longer financial planning periods than other systems. Forecasting income and expenditure is therefore more difficult and requires the use of more sophisticated methods than the usual annual budget. This chapter looks at the key problems and some of the management techniques for tackling them.

Forecasting costs and income

So, what is likely to be different in open systems? For some systems there will be little change. In others there will be a move from a system with largely variable costs to one with largely fixed costs. This is best explained by illustration.

Consider three systems. The first is a class-based system in which groups of learners are enrolled and where teachers are paid for the hours they teach. If there are enough learners to make a group, then the group runs. If there are too few learners, then the group is cancelled. I shall call this the traditional model. In this model (Figure 8.1) there is an initial low level of fixed costs (mostly the central staff who do no teaching). Further costs (the time of the teachers) are matched with further income (student fees). Costs and income rise in matched steps although, for simplicity, the steps are shown as straight lines on the figure.

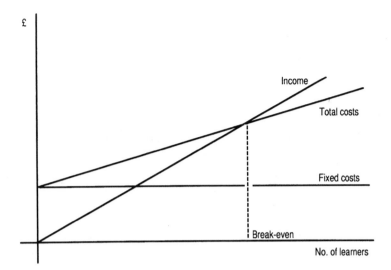

Figure 8.1   *The cost structure of a the traditional model*

Because the costs rise in steps alongside the small step increases in income, the balance is never far from break-even. In other words, with this type of model you are unlikely to ever make a big loss, or a big profit. It is a relatively low-risk model.

In the second, open system, an organization offers courses to individuals, using course materials bought from outside suppliers. As each person enrols, materials are bought for that person. Tutors are paid per learner that they take through a course. I shall call this the bought-in open model.

In this model (Figure 8.2) there is again an initial low level of fixed costs. Again teaching costs rise in line with enrolments, but this time the steps are even smaller – one step for each student.

Again, the straight line is never very far from the stepped line, showing that costs and income tend to rise together. It is another low-risk model.

In the third system, where the organization makes its own materials, there is a high level of fixed cost. Making materials usually takes more than one year so much of the fixed cost has to be paid before there are any enrolments. I shall call this the materials creation model.

Because there is now a large fixed cost, large numbers of learners are required before break-even is reached (Figure 8.3) but once break-even is reached, further enrolments yield a high margin. So, in the materials creation model, it is easy to make huge losses and also possible to make good profits. It is a very high-risk model.

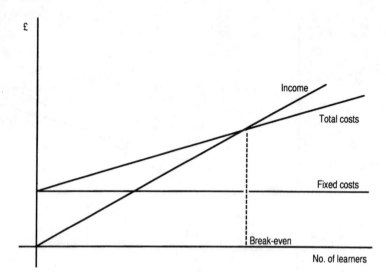

Figure 8.2   *The cost structure of the bought-in model*

Most organizations which start up open systems will have some experience of the traditional model. For example, colleges of higher education may wish to convert class-based courses to an open mode, or employers may need a flexible approach to replace class-based training. In each of these cases, a move to the

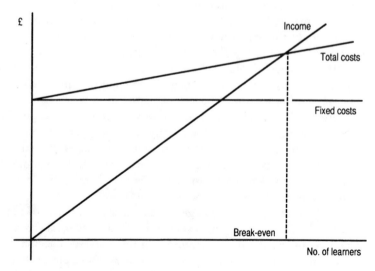

Figure 8.3   *The materials creation model*

bought-in model only requires small changes to the systems used for managing the finances of a class-based system. Moving to a materials creation model is quite another matter. Given the risks involved in these changes, what can be done to minimize them? The rest of this chapter explores some of the available methods.

Reducing the risks

The financial risks in a materials creation model are considerable (as evidenced by the large number of such schemes that have been and gone) and so need appropriate financial management expertise. What is that expertise?

The expertise needed to set up and run materials creation systems is a mixture of two things:

- market research
- investment appraisal.

Using market research to reduce risk

There is nothing that can be done within a financial management system to make something sell that people do not wish to buy. So, the first step to good financial planning is good market research. The greater the financial risk, the more extensive this research has to be and the more likely it is that expert help needs to be called in. Most new courses and systems start with one or two people who have a pretty good idea about what is wanted. In other words, market research is often used to confirm and refine hunches.

While on the one hand, market research is essential where there is any degree of financial risk, on the other hand it is easy to put too much faith in what it can tell us. This is for (at least) three reasons.

First, people do not necessarily know what they want, so asking them questions like, 'What kind of course would you like us to offer?' may not be helpful. After all, no one said that they wanted the Walkman. Nor was the Open University based on a market research specification. Despite this, both have been immensely successful.

Second, even when people know what they want, they may not be able to describe it sufficiently precisely to enable you to provide it.

Third, people have a tendency to say what they think the interviewer wants to hear, and to be optimistic in what they said. (In the early market research for The Open College, members of the public said they would pay well over £100 for a course. When courses were actually put on sale, it was hard to sell them at half this price.)

Does this mean market research is a waste of time? Not at all. It just means that it has to be conducted with care, checking at each stage of development that you are moving in the right direction. For example, focus groups can be used to:

- get initial ideas for what people want and why
- put course offerings and course concepts to people to get reactions to them
- test out marketing approaches.

Test marketing can be used as a final check before committing the production and marketing expenses.

If you wish to look at market research in more detail, a number of good sources are given in the further reading section.

Reducing risks through investment appraisal

Investment appraisal involves looking at a proposed investment and working out what type of financial return it can be expected to yield. The methods used take account of the fact that, if you receive £1,000 now, it is worth more than receiving £1,000 in a year's time. If you were to get the money now, then you could invest it and earn interest on it. For example, if interest rates were 7 per cent, then you would be £70 better off if you received the £1,000 now rather than in a year's time, as Table 8.1 shows.

Table 8.1 *Comparison of receiving £1,000 now or £1,000 in one year's time at an interest rate of 7 per cent*

Case	Money in hand now	Money in hand in one year's time
Case (a): receive £1,000 now	£1,000	£1,070
Case (b): receive £1,000 in one year's time	£0	£1,000

Generally, when you invest money in course development, you pay out money now in the hope of receiving income later. This raises two problems:

- you may be certain what your costs are, but forecasting sales or enrolments may involve a wide margin of error

- the money you receive in the future will be worth less to you than if you received it now.

The first problem has been discussed above under market research. The second problem, illustrated by Table 8.1, can be addressed by the methods discussed below. First, though, an example to illustrate why investment appraisal is important.

Example

A course costs £20,000 to develop. Learners are enrolled at a fee of £120 each. It costs £70 to teach each learner on the course, so each learner contributes £50 to paying back the development costs:

> Contribution to development costs = fee − cost of teaching the learner
>
> = £120 − 70 = £50.

There are 100 enrolments a year for four years, so the total contribution to development costs is:

> 400 learners × £50 = £20,000.

In other words, the course development cost is apparently recovered, as is illustrated in Table 8.2.

Table 8.2   *The apparent recovery of the development costs of a course*

Year	Costs and income	Costs and income £
Year 0	Cost of developing the course	−20000
Year 1	100 enrolments @ £50	+5000
Year 2	100 enrolments @ £50	+5000
Year 3	100 enrolments @ £50	+5000
Year 4	100 enrolments @ £50	+5000
Net profit/loss		0

In fact, Table 8.2 is misleading and this course is losing money. The income in column 3 has been treated as if £5,000 in one, two or three year's time is worth the same as having £5,000 now. For example, the £5,000 received from the year 2 students would have been worth far more if it had been received in year 0. Had it been received then, it would have earned two year's interest by year 2. If interest rates were, say, 7 per cent, that is £724.50 lost interest (£350 for the first year, and then 7 per cent of £5,350). Table 8.2 needs to be modified to show this lost interest. This is done using discounting factors from a discount table. The following explores this case in more detail.

Appraisal using discounted cash flow

Assuming again an interest rate of 7 per cent, we reduce the year 1 £5,000 by a factor of 0.935. (This factor is found from tables – you don't have to know how to work out discounting factors in order to apply these methods.) So, after discounting, the £5,000 becomes:

$$£5,000 \times 0.935 = £4,675.$$

What this says is that, if you had £4,675 now, then it would be worth £5,000 in one year's time.

For year 2, we need a discount factor which takes account of two years' lost interest. This factor is 0.873, so the year 2 £5,000 becomes:

$$£5,000 \times 0.873 = £4,365.$$

Table 8.3 shows Table 8.2 rewritten with all the discount factors put in. (We don't have to discount the year 0 costs since this is the base year to which all the other figures are being brought.) You can now see from column 5 that the net income after four years is −£3,065. A course that appeared to break even in Table 8.2, is really losing just over £3,000.

Appraising a course investment

The following is a summary of the steps to follow if you wish to apply the discounted cash flow method to one of your projects. The summary assumes that all the development costs occur in year 0, the year before enrolment income starts. If your investment costs are spread over more years, or continue to occur then you will need to consult a book such as Sizer (1989).

1.   Make a table with five columns as in Table 8.3.
2.   Label the first row below the headings as 'Year 0'.
3.   Label the remaining rows 'Year 1', 'Year 2', etc for as many years as you intend to use the course without any major new investment in it.

Table 8.3   *The cost recovery picture once the income is discounted*

Year (column 1)	Costs and income (column 2)	Costs and income £ (column 3)	Discount factor @ 7 per cent interest (column 4)	Discounted costs and income £ (column 5 = column 3 × column 4)
Year 0	Cost of developing the course	−20,000	1	−20,000
Year 1	100 enrolments @ £50	+5,000	0.935	+4,675
Year 2	100 enrolments @ £50	+5,000	0.873	+4,365
Year 3	100 enrolments @ £50	+5,000	0.816	+4,080
Year 4	100 enrolments @ £50	+5,000	0.763	+3,815
Net profit/loss		0		−3,065

4. Put your development cost into the year 0 row, remembering that it goes in as a negative number.
5. Put the contribution from fees into column 3. This is the profit that you make after the direct costs of teaching each learner. These are income figures, so they are positive.
6. Find out what rate of interest you could get on your money if you put it into a bank rather than developed the course. Put that rate at the top of column 4.
7. Find a set of discount factor tables (also called present value factors); see, for example, Sizer (1989, p.236).
8. In the table, look up the column for your interest rate. Copy the discount factors for each year into column 4.
9. Multiply the column 3 figures by the column 4 figures and put the result in column 5.
10. Add up column 5. A negative answer means that the course will make a loss. A positive answer means that the course will make a profit.

It is often best to do these calculations on a spreadsheet since:

- your spreadsheet may have built-in discount factors so you don't need to look them up in a table
- you can quickly see what happens with different interest rates

- you can quickly see what happens if the enrolment pattern is different, eg, you can compare four years of 50, 100, 150, 200 against four years of 100, 200, 150, 50.

This latter point emphasizes that one of the benefits of this method is that it allows you to see how sensitive your profit forecast is to changes in your forecast costs, forecast enrolment levels and forecast enrolment pattern. Table 8.4 shows how the data have to be laid out for Excel. The shaded box contains the formula:

$$= \text{NPV}(\$C\$1, D1:D8)$$

It is now easy to change the interest, the investment or the income and see what happens to the profit.

Table 8.4　*Spreadsheet chart for the data in Table 8.3*

	A	B	C
1		Interest rate =	0.07
2			
3	Year	Cost/income	Costs/income
4	Year 0	Development	−20,000
5	Year 1	100 enrolments @ £50	5,000
6	Year 2	100 enrolments @ £50	5,000
7	Year 3	100 enrolments @ £50	5,000
8	Year 4	100 enrolments @ £50	5,000
9	Discounted total		16,935
	Net profit		−3,065

Payback period appraisal

A simpler and somewhat cruder method of appraisal is to find the payback period, ie, 'How long will it take us to get our cash back?' The method has some value when comparing projects with the same investment level and when cashflow is a higher priority than profit. An example is the best way to explain the process.

Open to All has £20,000 to invest in a new course and has two courses under consideration: Word-processing and Spreadsheets. Their expected cashflows are as in Table 8.5.

Table 8.5   *Two possible course investments*

Year £	Word-processing £	Spreadsheets
0	−20,000	−20,000
1	8,000	2,000
2	7,000	3,000
3	6,000	6,000
4	3,000	7,000
5	2,000	8,000

The payback method finds the year in which the costs will have been recovered. Table 8.6 shows how this is done by inserting two additional columns to calculate how much of the investment is left to pay off at the end of each year. This shows that the word-processing course will be paid off during year 3 while the spreadsheet course will be paid off in year 5. So, although both courses have the same costs and income, the word-processing one is the better of the two investments since it recovers the investment more quickly.

Table 8.6   *Finding the payback years (shaded) for the two projects*

Year	Word-processing profit/loss	Cumulative	Spreadsheets profit/loss	Cumulative
0	−20,000	−20,000	−20,000	−20,000
1	8,000	−12,000	2,000	−18,000
2	7,000	−5,000	3,000	−15,000
3	6,000	+1,000	6,000	−9,000
4	3,000	+4,000	7,000	−2,000
5	2,000	+6,000	8,000	+6,000

Rate of return appraisal

Another way of thinking about investment appraisal is to ask what rate of return a particular project produces. For example, a project with investment costs of £100 and a year 1 income of £130 has a rate of return of 30 per cent:

$$\text{Rate of return} = \frac{\text{Profit}}{\text{Development costs}} = \frac{30}{100} = 30 \text{ per cent}$$

The rate of return is like the interest rate in a savings account. If a one-year project with development costs of £100 has a rate of return of 30 per cent, then that tells you that it gives the same profit as putting the £100 into a bank for one year at 30 per cent. The link with interest rates is important when making investment decisions since it does not make financial sense to run a project which has a rate of return below current deposit account interest rates. You might as well put the money in the bank.

So far, I have only shown how the rate of return is calculated for a one-year project. If the project runs over more than one year, you need to use discounted cash flows. To find the rate of return, you need to work as follows, using a computer spreadsheet program:

1. Set up your project table as in Table 8.7. The cell C9 contains the formula = NVP (C1, C5:C8). Cell C10 contains the calculation = sum (C9 + C4).
2. Enter an interest rate (say 0.1, ie, 10 per cent). This is just a starting guess. The computer will tell you whether you are too high or low.
3. Look at the figure in cell C10. If this figure is positive, try a higher rate of interest in place of your 10 per cent figure. If the figure in cell C10 is negative, try a lower rate of interest.
4. Continue trying interest rate values until you find the one that brings the net profit/loss figure to as near zero as you can get it.
5. This interest rate is the rate of return on the project.

Table 8.7 shows a project in which, using this method, an interest rate of 9.925 per cent reduces the net profit/loss to £1 which is near enough zero. So, we can say that the rate of return is 9.925 per cent. The project should not therefore be contemplated unless deposit rates are well below this figure. In practice, since any investment project carries more risk than putting money in a bank, a rate of return well above deposit rates will be looked for. Typically, organizations might seek rates of return of 20–30 per cent.

Table 8.7 *Data for a project in which the rate of return has been found to be 9.925 per cent*

	A	B	C
1		Interest rate =	0.09925
2			
3	Year	Cost/income	Costs/income £
4	Year 0	Development	−25,000
5	Year 1	160 enrolments @ £50	8,000
6	Year 2	200 enrolments @ £50	10,000
7	Year 3	160 enrolments @ £50	8,000
8	Year 4	100 enrolments @ £50	5,000
9	Discounted total		25,001
10	Net profit/loss		1

Chapter 9

Where next?

In this book I have suggested that there is a specific range of tasks which comprise the management of open systems. These tasks are over and above those of managing any system. Open systems therefore need managers of a high calibre, although not all managers need to be able to cover all aspects of open learning. In all but the smallest systems, there will be enough managers to allow for some specialization.

With this opportunity for specialization in mind, managers of open systems need to ask, 'Do we, as an organization, possess the skills that we need?' The following audit list is one way of beginning to answer this question. Where the answer is 'No', then a decision has to be made on how that skill might be acquired, through the development of a member of staff for example, or by purchasing the skill on those occasions when it is needed.

The audit list

Skill	Needed in the organization?	Present in the organization?
Design and management of pre-enrolment advice systems	☐	☐
Design and management of in-course information systems for learners	☐	☐
Design and management of enrolment systems	☐	☐
Selection and acquisition of appropriate learning materials, including kits	☐	☐
Storage and despatch of learning materials	☐	☐
The management of course maintenance	☐	☐
Managing the provision of access to laboratories	☐	☐
Managing the provision of access to computers	☐	☐
Managing the use of telephones for teaching and learning	☐	☐
Managing computer conferencing	☐	☐
Managing the use of fax for teaching and learning	☐	☐
Managing tutors as supporters of learning	☐	☐
Managing peer and group support systems	☐	☐

Managing the use of diagnostic tests	☐	☐
Managing the development and use of course guides	☐	☐
Managing the provision of information to tutors	☐	☐
Managing tutor development	☐	☐
Managing the development of other supporters	☐	☐
Managing assessed tutor-marked assignments	☐	☐
Managing computer-based tests	☐	☐
Managing online assessments	☐	☐
Managing examinations	☐	☐
Managing portfolio-based assessments	☐	☐
Managing negotiated assessments	☐	☐
Managing the provision of information on assessment	☐	☐
Managing the monitoring of learners and tutors	☐	☐
Managing action planning arising from monitoring	☐	☐
Managing evaluation	☐	☐
Managing the evaluation of materials	☐	☐
Managing quality systems	☐	☐
Managing investment	☐	☐

References

Baker, M (1983) 'The fast feedback system', *Teaching at a Distance*, 24.

Bates, AW (1995) *Technology, Open Learning and Distance Education*, London: Routledge.

Cole, GA (1993) *Management Theory and Practice*, 4th edn, London: DP Publications.

Davies, P and Gribble, L (1994) *Open School Good Practice Guide: Teletutoring via fax*, Dartington: The Open School Trust.

Department of Employment Training Agency (1990) *Ensuring Quality in Open Learning*, Sheffield: DoE.

Freeman, R (1992) *Quality Assurance in Training and Education: How to apply BS 5750 (ISO 9000) standards*, London: Kogan Page.

Freeman, R (1993) 'MAIL: from the NEC', *Teaching at a Distance*, 24.

Freeman, R (1996) *How to Become a Nursing Development Unit: A guide*, London: Kings Fund.

Hodgson, B (1993) *Key Terms and Issues in Open and Distance Learning*, London: Kogan Page.

HSE (1996) *COSHH Approved Code of Practice*, 2nd edn, London: Health and Safety Executive.

Jeffries, C *et al.* (1990) *The A–Z of Open Learning*, Cambridge: National Extension College.

Jennison, K (1996) *CoSy Takes the Distance Out of Distance Learning*, London: Open University, London Region.

Jones, A, Kirkup, G and Kirkwood, A (1992) *Personal Computers for Distance Education: The study of an educational innovation*, London: Paul Chapman.

Kolb, MK (1990) *The Adult Learner: A neglected species*, 4th edn, Houston, TX: Gulf Publishing.

Lewis, R (1995) *Tutoring in Open Learning*, Lancaster: Framework Press.

Mansfield, C and Robertson, S (1996) 'Developing Internet couseware to create freedom and flexibility for learners in university English studies', in Wisdom, Pollard, Downey, Rao and Slater (eds) *Deliberations*, London: Guildhall and Kingston.

Mason, R (1994) *Using Communications Media in Open and Flexible Learning*, London: Kogan Page.

Mullett, T (1983) 'Feedback on T101', *Teaching at a Distance*, 24.

Perrin, M (1992) 'VIFAX: learning a foreign language at a distance', *Open Learning*, 7, 1, 48–9.

Rickwood, P (1994) 'Some Open University students' experience of transfer', *Open Learning*, 9, 2, 23–8.

Rowntree, D (1991) *Statistics without Tears*, Harmondsworth: Penguin.

Rowntree, D (1992) *Exploring Open and Distance Learning*, London: Kogan Page.

RSA (nd) *Training and Development Award Suite: Centre Support Pack*, London: RSA Examinations Board.

Sizer, J (1989) *An Insight into Management Accounting*, 3rd edn, Harmondsworth: Penguin.

Thorpe, M (1993) *Evaluating Open and Distance Learning*, 2nd edn, Harlow: Longman.

Further reading

General

Hodgson, B (1993) *Key Terms and Issues in Open and Distance Learning,* London: Kogan Page.
> A useful guide to terminology in open learning. The explanations are long enough to give some practical 'how to do it' detail.

Jeffries, C *et al.* (1990) *The A–Z of Open Learning,* Cambridge: National Extension College.
> Similar to Hodgson (1993) but has more, but shorter entries.

Lewis, R (1985) *How to Develop and Manage an Open-learning Scheme.* London: Council for Educational Technology.
> One of the first practical guides to setting up a scheme. Still contains much useful detail.

Lewis, R and Freeman, R (1994) *Open Learning in Further and Higher Education: A staff development programme.* Lancaster: Framework Press.
> A set of workshop exercises for open learning staff. Covers most aspects of setting up a new scheme.

Mansfield, C (1995) *'Poetica: Programme for Orientation, Education and Telematics Implementation in Critical Analysis'*, unpublished paper, University of Sunderland.

Mansfield, C (1996) *'Designing outcome-driven independent learning materials for the World Wide Web'*, unpublished paper, University of Sunderland.

Rowntree, D (1992) *Exploring Open and Distance Learning,* London: Kogan Page.
> A good overview of just about every aspect of open learning.

Finance

Rumble, G (1997) *Costs and Economics of Open Distance Learning,* London: Kogan Page.
Sizer, J (1989) *An Insight into Management Accounting,* 3rd edn, Harmondsworth: Penguin.
A well-established guide to accounting. Although written for students, this book is highly accessible to the general manager.

Marketing

Hunter, I and Beeson, D (nd) *Marketing Open and Flexible Learning*, Dunstable, NATFHE Open Learning Section.
Mostly about selling open learning courses by direct mail.

Materials development

Dean, C and Whitlock, Q (1993) *A Handbook of Computer-Based Training*, London: Kogan Page.
Freeman, R and Lewis, R (1995) *Writing Open Learning Materials: Staff Development Activities for FE and HE*, Lancaster: Framework Press.
Race, P (1994) *The Open Learning Handbook*, 2nd edn, London: Kogan Page.
Rowntree, D (1990) *Teaching Through Self-Instruction*, London: Kogan Page.
Rowntree, D (1994) *Preparing Materials for Open, Distance and Flexible Learning: An Action Guide for Teachers and Learners*, London: Kogan Page.

Market research

Chisnall, PM (1991) *The Essence of Marketing Research,* New York: Prentice Hall.
A useful introduction to the subject.
Worcester, R and Downham, J (eds) (1986) *Consumer Market Research Handbook,* Maidenhead: McGraw-Hill.
A fund of expertise on marketing. Very readable and practical. Several chapters have immediate application to education and training market research: Chapter 1 (Nigel Newson Smith) on desk research; Chapter 2 (Peter Sampson) on qualitative research and motivation research; Chapter 5 (J Marton-Williams) on questionnaire design; Chapter 6 (John F Drakeford and Valerie Farbridge) on interviewing and field control; Chapter 10 (Leonard England and Peter Arnold) on telephone, mail and other techniques; and Chapter 15 (Colin Greenhalgh) on research for new product development.

Monitoring and evaluation

Calder, J (1994) *Programme Evaluation and Quality,* London: Kogan Page.
> Deals with evaluating programmes (rather than courses). Invaluable if that is what you need to evaluate.

Rowntree, D (1991) *Statistics without Tears,* Harmondsworth: Penguin.
> If you need to use or understand statistics, this is a good place to start.

Thorpe, M (1993) *Evaluating Open and Distance Learning,* 2nd edn, Harlow: Longman.
> This book provides a good survey of the issues that you might consider for monitoring and evaluation and discusses a wide range of examples of how the data might be collected. Most of the examples are taken from the Open University and, in parts of the book, the lack of consideration of other systems is a serious weakness.

Standards

RSA (1995) *Training and Development Award Suite: Centre support pack,* London: RSA Examinations Board.
> This pack provides a comprehensive explanation of the training and development standards and of the RSA awards that are based on these. Section 8, the national standards, is the part most relevant to the issues discussed in this book.

Quality assurance

British Standards Institution (1987) *BS 5750 Part 0,* London: BSI. The UK standard for quality assurance systems.
> This has now been replaced by the ISO 9000 series.

Department of Employment Training Agency (1990) *Ensuring Quality in Open Learning,* Sheffield: Department of Employment Training Agency.
> Still the bible for quality in open learning.

Freeman, R (1993) *Quality Assurance in Training and Education,* London: Kogan Page.
> A guide to how to apply BS 5750/ISO 9000 to training and education.

Sallis, E (1996) *Total Quality Management in Education,* 2nd edn, London: Kogan Page.

Saturn Quality Working Group (1992) *Saturn Quality Guide for Open and Distance Learning,* Amsterdam: Saturn Quality Working Group.
> The EU alternative to Department of Employment Training Agency (1990).

Tutorial skills and tutor development

Lewis, R (1995) *Tutoring in Open Learning*, Lancaster: Framework Press.

This is a set of workshop activities for training tutors in open learning skills. It is a key resource for anyone setting up a new open learning system or making substantial changes to the tutoring of an existing scheme. Topics covered include: defining your role; commenting on written work and giving feedback; tutoring by telephone; face-to-face tutoring; using a computer [in tutoring]; underlying tutorial skills; working with learning materials. The section on telephone tutoring is a major contribution to the literature on this method of teaching.

Open College, The (1991) *Staff Development in Open Learning: Tutoring Learners*. The Blueprint Series, Manchester: The Open College (1991).

A very practical approach to tutoring skills

SCOTTSU (1990) *Training Course in Tutoring Open Learning Schemes*, SCOTTSU International Ltd, Gardyne Road, Broughton Ferry, Dundee, Tayside DD5 1NY. Tel: 01382 454438; fax: 01382 454921.

A distance learning course in open learning tutoring skills. The course may be taken with SCOTTSU, or the materials can be purchased for use in another organization.

Index